THE OPEN UNIVERSITY
A Second Level Interdisciplinary Course
Art and Environment

unit 12
body, mind, stage and street

Prepared for the course team by Susan Triesman

The Open University Press

The Open University Press
Walton Hall, Milton Keynes

First published 1976

Designed by the Media Development Group of the Open University.

Produced in Great Britain by
Technical Filmsetters Europe Limited, 76 Great Bridgewater Street, Manchester M1 5JY

ISBN 0 335 06211 3

This text forms part of an Open University course. The complete list of units in the course appears at the end of this text.

For general availability of supporting material referred to in this text please write to the Director of Marketing, The Open University, PO Box 81, Milton Keynes, MK7 6AT.

Further information on Open University courses may be obtained from the Admissions Office, The Open University, PO Box 48, Milton Keynes, MK7 6AB.

1.1

CONTENTS

The television programmes 'Anyone Can Dance' and 'Community Theatre' are connected with this unit.

The unboxed marginal comments are extracts from Richard Orton's assessment of this unit.

TOMORROW AND TOMORROW AND TOMORROW...

Possessors of the new supersize television screen spent a stimulating evening yesterday in witnessing the most recent work of Owen Caig, whose growing mastery of the atmospheric values of mountain vistas has already won him his eminence as one of the foremost exponents of modern drama. His crystalline evocation of three-dimensional space recalls some of Leonardo da Vinci's scenic backgrounds in the 'Mona Lisa' and the 'Virgin with Saint John'. The play, ranging as it did from the Apennines to the Andes, afforded admirable scope for Mr Caig's dramatic climaxes. Such actors as were necessary to provide the compositional balance for these superb theatrical compositions remained appropriately in the background, never obtruded themselves, and in no way interfered with the meaning of the play.*

The success of the mass drama Eons and Ions at the Civic Arena continues unabated. After the concluding liturgy, 842 persons in the audience announced their conversion and were immediately ordained in the new faith in the presence of the chorus and the entire cast.*

We went to the Endless Theatre again, yesterday. It's the ideal place for a Bank Holiday. We boarded our pony chariot on the roof at Bourne and Hollingsworth, got our multiprogramme and went off to join the race. Actually, I always think that first part is the most fascinating, you know: as you speed along the racetrack over the department stores, and then over the City, and into the countryside. You get so much understanding of how people live from those close-angled glimpses into their bedrooms and gardens. However, to get to the main items: we dropped the children off at the Great Lido, promising to pick them up later at the Beatific Baseball Stadium. Then we were free to have our normal argument about what to do ourselves. Fred wanted to watch the All-Universe shot-put contests in the Superstadium, and I wanted to see Climactic Cinema's re-run of the great moments of the 30 000 best films of the 90s. It had such good thought-ups in the transference session last Sunday. We compromised, as usual, by settling for a double swivel waterbed in the Video Variety Hall, where we could both see everything (including keeping an eye on the children) and zoom in when things got interesting. I was quite exhausted when we left, but I'm sure you'll be pleased to know we won a prize coming home for the best performance in the race over Balham.†

From our Decisional Commentator:

There were exciting scenes in the House last night in the performance over the Parsimony Bill. Lord Peruguay, Acting Home Secretary (on loan from the Inter-Moslem Alliance for the summer season) succeeded, against all predictions, in getting the bill rejected by an enormous demonstration. He utilized a mixture of truth drugs and consciousness synthesizers to expose the appalling fantasies lying behind the lies of both the government and the opposition. At one point, the control from the audience became very heated, as they all switched into the thought-streams and memory impulses of the Minister for Aid. The screens were completely blackened within seconds by a dense cloud of prejudice. The hall had to be cleared to let in some fresh air, and during this intermission, the Minister managed to make good his escape.

The temper of the crowd was leading up to a violent end, and he just was not prepared to take responsibility for his acts. We understand from his senior staff that he has taken refuge in one of the anti-theatre sanctuaries run by the old Lip-reading Party. If this is true, it will finish his career.

* From Lee Simonson (1932) *The Stage is Set*, Theatre Arts Books, 1963, pp. 10–11.

† Projection of a projection by Susan Triesman of Frederick Kiesler's proposal for Endless Theatre in the mid 1920s.

When the performance resumed, it was but a formality to kill the bill for increased parsimony towards the Nineteenth World, and Lord Peruguay dematerialized to report to the World Decisional Theatre in its new travelling stadium.

Many of the audience/participators were treated with first aid as a result of the excitement, and experts will spend today repairing the electronic circuits blown by last night's revelations.*

2020

At the routine end of the decade check-up at the St Martin's yesterday, the doctor-in-charge discovered that the entire cast and audience of *The Mousetrap* had mortified into fixed positions as of the end of scene two. On later examination by a team of pathologists, the people involved were declared to have been dead for at least eight years. The West End Theatres Confederacy has decided to leave them like that in perpetuity, since it will not affect the run of the play, and the Arts Council has agreed to continue paying the subsidy for the upkeep of this national institution. This paper welcomes this decision in the name of the preservation of both the presence and values of the Great Bourgeois Epoch.*

PROLOGUE

On 30 May 1967 theatre in Greece came to an abrupt halt. The junta imposed censorship. They were very thorough about it, censoring both the text and, by alterations following attendance at dress rehearsals, the performance. Their criteria were as follows:

All theatrical pieces, or musicals and public shows of any kind, are forbidden which:

1   disturb or could disturb public order;

2   propagate subversive theories;

3   defame our country nationally or touristically;

4   undermine the healthy social traditions of the Greek people and their ancestral habits and customs;

5   Touch on Christian religion;

6   attack the person of the King, the members of the Royal Family, and the government;

7   exercise a distorting influence on the aesthetic evolution of the people.

This circular, signed by Papadopoulos, was clear in its determination not to impose restrictions on the art 'whose cradle has been this country from time immemorial' but to prevent only cheap and corrupting speculations.

From that moment to the end of the Colonels' Regime, the plays which, to borrow the phrase, had cradled the art of theatre were all banned. The plays of Aeschylus, Sophocles, Euripides — the great classic tragedies — were all found to be potentially disruptive: far too political to be presented. They are all concerned, in one way or another, with the relationship between the individual and the state. Indeed, if you examine the great tragedies of Western theatre, you will find that this is a common underlying theme. People who condemn 'political theatre' as an outrage on the body of a respectably otherwise-oriented art form are denying the essence of theatre: its (to use existentialist terminology) being-in-the-world. Theatre is the most public of all the arts and it takes for its themes all that concerns human society. There is no such thing as 'pure' entertainment.

* Projections by Susan Triesman.

The question as to what constitutes theatre — what it does and is — is a muscular ghost, haunting all writing on the subject. The factors that make it difficult to answer have been multiplied by the increasing difficulty in drawing lines between theatre and other art forms — even, in some cases, between theatre and life. We may none of us ever find the ultimate definition, but the quest is rewarding. It allows us to examine individually the cluster of ideas, things, events, people and places that make up theatre, and understand their inter-relationships.

APOLOGY

Having entered on such a grandiose note, let me deflate it immediately. The task of defining theatre in its totality and in all its parts, while highly desirable, would be impossible within the limits of this unit. So long as we are, rightly, concerned with project work rather than with reading, some subjects must of necessity receive a less full treatment than others: some will be represented only by nods and winks and hints, and the hope that at some later date you may find time to research them in more detail for yourself. I simply cannot describe the whole history and theory of world theatre, but some parts of it will emerge as they illuminate specific developments or ideas. And since I am concentrating on examining theatre through ideas about it, I am not quoting extracts from plays. But I hope that you will read as many plays as possible.

A NOTE ON PROJECTS

While you may, if you wish, go straight to the projects and start work on them, I would like to emphasize that:

1   The improvisational work might provide useful material for other projects. As this may be an unexpected event, if unfamiliar to you as a technique for developing playwriting, for instance, I suggest that you try some of the work in that section before undertaking the other projects.

2   You should take note of the ways in which theatre and society interact, and be aware of this while doing the projects.

There are also some specifically background projects scattered throughout the text. They act as a kind of subtext and should be used as a means of enlarging your consideration of theatre, extending definitions, finding ways to put your personal perceptions into a form that might be translated into something else, whether theory or practice. Most of these subtextual projects take the form of questions. Your collection of answers or responses to them may clarify your choice of project work.

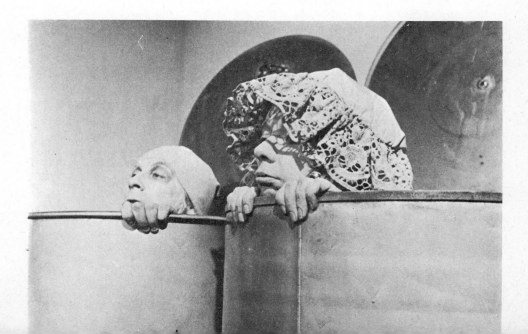

1 BACKCLOTH AND BASICS

Theatre can do without scenery, lighting, directors, buildings, even plays. The improvised play in an improvised street setting contains within it the essence of theatre. Some people claim that the audience is optional, especially those who create happenings in which everyone is a participant. However, in this case, I think we can say that each person attending the event is both actor and audience.

And for some people theatre is a particular form of drama, for others an event, for yet others a cultural phenomenon or a body of work. The answer to the question as to what theatre is and is for must come from a consideration of the intrinsic requirements of theatre: at least, this stripping-down process is a sound first stage.
What can theatre not do without?
Actors and audience.

A many-headed monster: The audience

Let us start by considering what going to the theatre is *like*. Well, for a start, it is like nothing at all for 98 per cent of the population of the United Kingdom. The majority of people simply do not attend theatres. Now, do not rush to conclusions — the statistic does not mean that they have never been to a performance. It means that only 2 per cent of the population makes a practice of going to Theatre with a capital T. The statistics do not generally include pantomime at Christmas, the variety show on the pier during the summer holiday, watching innumerable plays on television or listening to them on radio. The researchers seem to be guided by an idea of Theatre as residing in one spot, namely the traditional theatre building. It is a good enough place to start, so long as we also qualify the findings.

The findings: of the 2 per cent of regular Theatre-goers, the majority have been very well educated and are predominantly middle class. The opera is more the preserve of the upper middle class. Some of the few studies that exist (the small number puts us under a disadvantage as research becomes more of a projection than usual from the 'facts') have gone into more detail, revealing

the social as well as the class nature of theatre attendance. Many theatre-goers have a meal out, or an extended coffee session after the play. And they dress up for the occasion. In other words, theatre-going is, largely, a social ritual perpetuated by the middle and upper middle classes, and the play or show is only part of the evening's entertainment, which also includes an element of display.

We must also note that most shows open rather too early for less affluent or leisured people to get home after work, wash and get out to the centre of town in time to see them. And the prices are rather steep, considering the bad view you have in many parts of most theatres.

We must also note a fact not revealed by the statistics, but sworn to by managers and ticket agencies. In summer, theatres are almost full of tourists. Tourists, in effect, keep them open.

Here is a native cultural phenomenon: and there is an influx of outsiders. What can an anthropological approach to the subject yield on this contradiction? It might suggest a number of things: of which the most important might be that,

since the show is only *part* of the ritual, the *content* of the show is not terribly important. Therefore outsider and native can partake on almost equal terms in the social ritual of being seen in fashionable places, acquiring a particular status or self-authentication by so doing, demonstrating their part in the order of things. In this light it is interesting to recall that most people talk of going to *see* a play, in England, while in France they go to *assist at* it, and in North America, they *take it in*. Both the French and the American versions are more comprehensive than the English. What the audience is like is very pertinent to the show on the night: they do assist, not just sit passively. And the element of acquisition, the almost dietary overtones of the conspicuous consumption of leisure summoned up by *taking the show in*, is very clear. Anthropologist or critic apart, however, it cannot be denied that going to the theatre is a complex series of events and pieces of behaviour which *include* the play, but of which the play is *not* the only object. This seems to me to have much to do with the pass (and it is not a pretty one) that conventional theatre has reached. It is overwhelmed by the boring, the revivals of revivals, the re-worked, the meaningless parade of 'stars' demonstrating their virtuosity against the most mediocre backgrounds: what Peter Brook christened 'the deadly theatre'. It is this deadening thing which has happened to theatre, to the native culture, that allows the tourist intervention in the tribal rite to appear so natural.

Of course there are other people in the audience and there always have been. From ancient Greece until comparatively recently, theatre embraced all classes. The Roman emperors watched the games they had set up to keep the people quiet. The mimes and troubadours who kept the theatre traditions alive during the periods when it was banned (from the fourth to the ninth century AD, roughly) played on the village common for the ordinary people, and in the halls for the lords. Shakespeare's work derived much of its vitality from the healthy contradictions of a court audience on the one hand, and the mixture of nobles with groundlings and stinkards at the theatre on the other. In the eighteenth century the footmen's gallery was frequently cited as an image of the liberty enjoyed by the English. Indeed everybody except for the destitute or the very poor was a candidate for theatre-going, and it has become a cliché to point to the way the interior of the theatre reflected, upside-down, the very structure of society. Although opera was always priced out of the pocket of all but the richest, it was not until the nineteenth century that audiences were seriously divided into different buildings for their entertainment. The theatres of the middle classes survive, but the majority of music halls have long since been converted into cinemas and then bingo halls, if they have not been demolished.

And so the 2 per cent gained their own place for theatre. Plus the tourist element. The practice of visiting theatres abroad is an ancient and honourable one, as memoirs of Grand Tours demonstrate. We owe our only drawing of an Elizabethan theatre (the Swan) to a visiting Dutchman, Johann de Witt. The contemporary development of these visits is the international theatre festival. There are two varieties of this: the conventional, weighed down with worthy old masterpieces, and the alternative, an arena for the cross-fertilization of ideas and techniques. The effectiveness of the latter can be seen in the development of international theatre languages. As for the former, the living heritage is a worthy idea, but it seems to weigh altogether too heavily in the balance which decides on subsidies. Theatre is a living art form, and its vitality, not its preservation in aspic, should be encouraged. Change — not for its own sake, but organic change — is what keeps both people and their art forms alive.

So long as theatre needs subsidy and there is money for it, I say, Down with museums, and repeal the inequity of distribution of subsidies between the National Theatre, Covent Garden, the Royal Shakespeare, and the rest.

How does this question of subsidy relate to the audience? Conventional theatre is very expensive to produce, but its increasing costs are not equalled by increasing audiences. This means that conventional theatre does not like to take great risks; even when it is subsidized it is necessary to play safe, play for reassurance, and assure a full house. But we are living through a great upsurge in theatrical activity and discovery, most of which takes place outside conventional theatre. New audiences are being created, new forms being invented, new possibilities evolved. And while it is true that initially it can be very challenging and helpful to have to work on the proverbial shoestring, after some years it can have a detrimental effect, locking the experimenters into a form they reject but cannot afford to alter. And if you work with the intention of making theatre available to people who cannot afford West End prices, then you cannot charge enough to cover your costs: sudsidy is necessary. One of the Arts Council's terms of reference is the creation and extension of audiences: the way they spend the money available seems loaded in the direction of maintaining the traditional audience.

Rogues, vagabonds and realists: The players

Some of the basic attributes of acting are universally shared, and it is this universality which allows them to form a communication system. However, the way that professional acting builds on the universals changes over history.

The professional player emerged in England from the combination of mystery plays and minstrelsy, and later found protection under noblemen against the vagrancy acts which, referring to that background, categorized him among rogues and vagabonds. The rejection of players as citizens was common in Europe, and related to their mobility. The authorities, up to the period leading up to the Industrial Revolution, discouraged people from moving from their place of origin since it was easier to keep control if people stayed, literally, in their place. On the move they represented a threat to stable order. In addition to this, as puritanism became stronger, its antagonism to all forms of pleasure-giving gained ground. There was always a special place in hell for the actor,

whose wiles were a lure into corruption. The theatres of Elizabethan London were closed by the city fathers whenever there was an outbreak of plague; fair enough, as gatherings of people spread the disease. But they remained closed for months after the plague had died down, and here we can see links between puritanism and the battle for the control of London, as against the claims of the court. Acting was one of the chief pleasures of the court, and delays in reopening theatres were a gesture of defiance and control. During the Commonwealth, theatre was banned, and when Charles II restored theatres at the time of his restoration, some of the puritans may have begun to regret the pre-civil war version. The king and his retinue had imported continental ideas of theatre, and the new shape (the beginnings of the proscenium arch) and a certain amount of luxury evolved into a form where the ruling classes could view themselves both in the play and in the auditorium. The plays reflected the morals of the court, and the presence of actresses condemned them further. It was the close reflection that was probably the worst sin: plays mirrored the times too accurately.

It is well known that each age has claimed its great players as great *realists*, and has regarded with scorn the strange tastes of its predecessors. The past seems full of ranting, wooden gestures, artificiality. Seen (unfairly) in the scratchy hints of very old film, Sarah Bernhardt appears to be undeniably ham. But she was agreed by all to be one of the greatest actresses of all time, with the ability to make the very flesh of the audience suffer with her own. She produced a reality more real than reality:

> She was Phèdre or Marguerite Gautier . . . the actual woman, and she was also that other actual woman, Sarah Bernhardt. Two magics met and united. . . . There was an excitement in going to the theatre; one's pulses beat feverishly before the curtain had risen; there was almost a kind of obscure sensation of peril. . . . And the acting was a passionate declaration, offered to someone unknown; it was as if the whole nervous force of the audience were sucked out of it and flung back, intensified, upon itself, as it encountered the single, insatiable, indomitable nervous force of the woman. And so, in its way, this very artificial acting seemed the mere instinctive, irresistible expression of a temperament; it mesmerized one, awakening the senses and sending the intelligence to sleep.
> (Arthur Symons, 1909, *Plays, Acting and Music*, Constable, pp. 18–19.)

 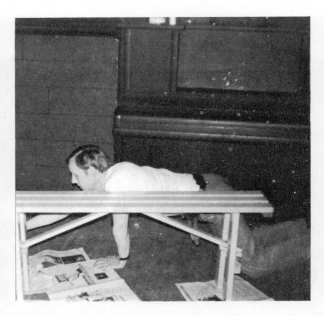 

It is interesting, in the light of Brecht's theories, that Symons insists that her greatness lay in not subsuming the actress entirely in the character. He also praised Irving for a different kind of acting, which seemed realistic through the evidence of intention in the acting, while it kept 'nature or the too close resemblance of nature, carefully out of his composition.' (ibid. p. 53.) Irving's was not art but science; it represented the old school, while Eleanora Duse, who lived her parts, represented the new. The divine Sarah, presumably, had found the happy medium. Now, all this raises questions about functions of acting. The idea that the player should, as nearly as possible, live the part seems to have developed alongside romanticism. But that statement begs another question about how reality itself was agreed upon as real. When David Garrick ousted the old style of heroic bombast, his performance was really news. People flocked to the unfashionable end of town to see the master of reality. His rival, Macklin, who never attained the same sort of popularity although attempting to create realistic actions on stage, had a greater influence on the following generations. He actually trained and rehearsed young actors at a time when the normal practice was for them to repeat the way the part had always been played, down to the least gesture. And that was considered realistic, because it was the correct tradition.

> Every character in the piece, first received its peculiar bias from its original representative; and hundreds who never saw Mr King, are pretty sure of seeing some of Mr King's manner, whenever they see *Sir Peter Teazle* on the stage: it is much the same with all the other parts we see done. The authors draw the outlines, and form the leading characteristics; but the peculiar, and personal qualities of the original performer go down to posterity, as a necessary and absolute portion of the said character.
> (Henry Lee, 1830, *Memoirs of a Manager*)

Contradictions are emerging. Garrick produces a new vision of a part; success justifies it; countless imitations follow it. The actor's originality, then, is not the source of the success, but his ability to apply some universal idea of behaviour to the part: the correct dose of contemporary psychology. Fanny Burney wrote about his ease and vivacity on stage, the 'fire and meaning in his eyes! — I could hardly believe he had studied a written part, for every word seemed to be uttered from the impulse of the moment.... Every look speaks!' (*Evelina*, Letter 10, 1778.) But what did every look say when assiduously copied by the next person playing the part? And what was the effect of a new style of

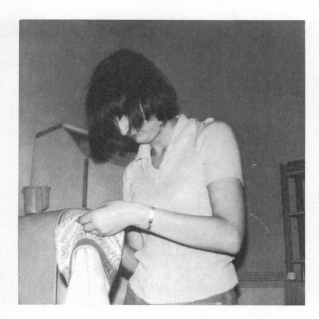

acting, based on a different understanding of human behaviour, on the other actors? Apparently it made the stage reality all too like reality itself:

> I was at Edinburgh one year when she was electrifying the Northern metropolis with many characters, and none more than this. One of her

fellow-performers, Mr Russell, told me an instance of her power in the part. A poor fellow who played the *Surveyor* in 'Henry VIII' was met by Mr Russell coming off the stage having just received the *Queen Katherine's* (Siddons's) rebuke; *'You were the Duke's surveyor, and lost your office on the complaint o' the tenants.'* The mimetic unjust steward was perspiring with agitation. 'What is the matter with you?' said Mr Russell. 'The matter?' quoth the other, 'that woman plays as if the thing were in earnest. She looked on me through and through with her black eyes, that I would not for the world meet her on the stage again.'

(James Boaden, *c.* 1825, *Life of Mrs Siddons*)

The eighteenth-century theatre was renowned for its great acting and its appalling plays: the actors needed enormous powers if they were to make the material come to life. They were acclaimed as realists when their creative method came closest to ongoing psychological concepts.

Thus the great moments of sudden transition between passions, for which Garrick and Macklin were famous, fitted the idea that there were ten passions which could be named and which had fixed modes of expression. Moving from one to another was the art.

The poor steward terrified by Siddons recognized what she was doing as being close to reality. Artists have been seen over the ages to pre-cognize changes in perception which later become theory: they break through received notions towards the change in feeling. Stanislavsky's theories demonstrate this change, and his own acting demonstrated the theories. But the new truths arrived at then have now become museum descriptions of an age long past. They no longer serve their original function. Stanislavsky was intent that the actor create life and truth on stage: truth of character comes from understanding the character and having the ability to call on one's own emotional and physical resources. In that way, the actor cannot help but make the play contemporary (since he uses his contemporary self) while at the same time remaining true to the intention of the author (through studying the play). It should not be possible for a different actor to repeat exactly the work of the one before.

But what does truth on stage mean? Or realism? Sarah Bernhardt's ability to mesmerize the audience was precisely the kind of acting that Brecht considered untruthful: rather than the narcotic effect of such vicarious living through another, theatre realism should tell the truth about life. Aristotle's concept of catharsis has been distorted. It derived from the real stage of his day: his *Poetics* is an aesthetic theory derived from actuality. And when he wrote it Greek actors were performing to crowds of 30 000, using masks and high heels and special ways of speaking in order to get the message across. No question of what *we* consider realism there...? Brecht was to return to the use of masks as one of the alienation techniques he advocated to prevent identification and mesmerization taking place. For Brecht, the art of acting was to stay outside the character, comment on it, perform, as it were, in quotes. His realism is that of facing up to reality, as if conducting an experiment. The spectator's recognition of the conditions displayed as real happens with astonishment, not complacency. 'This astonishment', says Walter Benjamin, 'is the means whereby epic theatre, in a hard, pure way, revives a Socratic praxis. In one who is astonished, interest is born: interest in its primordial form.' ('What is Epic Theatre' *Understanding Brecht*, 1973, New Left Books, p. 4.)

The rebels - whose aim is to overthrow the Chad Govt - have held her captive 17 months.

Most actors in the West derive their technique from Stanislavsky, whatever the name given to the method they learn. Including the Method, which yielded some very good actors and many more who could not be heard, so immersed were they in creating their own reality. Most of the experiments in recent years have been attempts to take Stanislavsky or Brecht to extremes, or even to unite them. Jerzy Grotowski's work in his Theatre Laboratory does this. His actors are trained as the most highly skilled physical instruments, capable of expressing anything with an intensity capable of producing revelations. The character of the revelations, while having the depth of religious archetypes, with political, social and personal undertones, is a way of making people face up to themselves.

The improvisation games in this unit, though they all trace their ancestry to Stanislavsky, are particularly useful for Brechtian acting. Indeed, unless you know how to create psychological and physical reality on stage, it is difficult to try to play against them.

Acting is a very powerful art form. The magnetism of great performers lingers over time, and people are partisan about their stars. Stage-door Johnnies have been replaced by gruelling miles of intimate detail in newspapers: we tut-tut over the latest divorce where they actively helped to produce it. One famous actress in the early eighteenth century, Mrs Bracegirdle, was the unwitting cause of duels. And no wonder, when not only was she a great beauty but

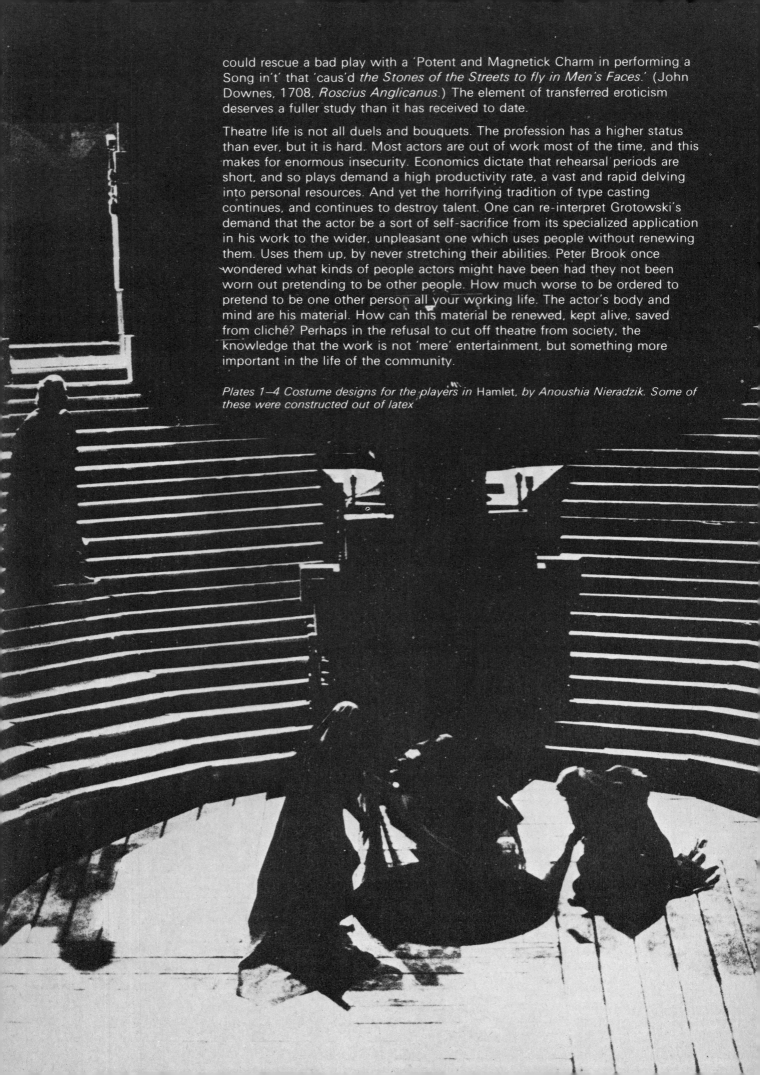

could rescue a bad play with a 'Potent and Magnetick Charm in performing a Song in't' that 'caus'd *the Stones of the Streets to fly in Men's Faces.*' (John Downes, 1708, *Roscius Anglicanus*.) The element of transferred eroticism deserves a fuller study than it has received to date.

Theatre life is not all duels and bouquets. The profession has a higher status than ever, but it is hard. Most actors are out of work most of the time, and this makes for enormous insecurity. Economics dictate that rehearsal periods are short, and so plays demand a high productivity rate, a vast and rapid delving into personal resources. And yet the horrifying tradition of type casting continues, and continues to destroy talent. One can re-interpret Grotowski's demand that the actor be a sort of self-sacrifice from its specialized application in his work to the wider, unpleasant one which uses people without renewing them. Uses them up, by never stretching their abilities. Peter Brook once wondered what kinds of people actors might have been had they not been worn out pretending to be other people. How much worse to be ordered to pretend to be one other person all your working life. The actor's body and mind are his material. How can this material be renewed, kept alive, saved from cliché? Perhaps in the refusal to cut off theatre from society, the knowledge that the work is not 'mere' entertainment, but something more important in the life of the community.

Plates 1–4 Costume designs for the players in Hamlet, *by Anoushia Nieradzik. Some of these were constructed out of latex*

2 THE SISTER ARTS, AND OTHER RELATIONS

Bricks, mortar and magic

Before we can examine the visual and spatial theatre arts, we must look at the space in which they normally operate.

When you mention the word 'theatre' to people, the predominant image summoned up is that of a theatre building — a particular one with a proscenium arch, a roof, an elliptical auditorium, circles and boxes, bars, a foyer, plush red seating and gilt decorations. In other words, the theatre as left over by the nineteenth century, itself a muddle of legacies ... and very uncomfortable, on the whole. Someone always seems to be intolerably tall in front of you, or unjustly fat on either side. The red plush richness is offset by the stingy narrowness of your allotted space.

> The nineteenth century has left our cities stuffed with pestiferous playgoer barrels in which the unfortunate playwright and actors were expected by sheer force of entertaining power to set up an attraction that would counterbalance the greatest discomfort of the greatest number.
> (E. J. West, ed., 1958, *Shaw on Theatre*, Hill & Wang, p. 177)

The amazing docility of the audiences in the face of such arrangements adds to the annoyance.

> If criminals were crowded together in our prisons without proper ventilation and elbow room, as playgoers are in our theatres, there would be an agitation against the cruelty of the authorities.
> (*Shaw on Theatre*, p. 178)

Why should theatre be uncomfortable? It is largely the result of history and economics. The first Drury Lane theatre held several hundred people, the third, a century later, held over 3000 spectators. The more people crammed in, the more money taken. Why is it important to consider the actual buildings? I just used the word spectators instead of audience

Chickens and eggs

The dramatic works that have come down to us from history bear witness to the impact of particular theatre forms — shapes and spaces — on the way the play is written. The building cannot be considered in isolation from its function, and the plays and procedures of theatre cannot be considered in isolation from the place that houses them. But which came first?

When asked about his approach to directing the classics, the Greek director Minotis said that the theatre at Epidaurus was the best teacher. By standing on the acting area or in the auditorium he could discover most of what he needed to know about the necessities of the production. But we have no way of knowing whether the huge amphitheatres carved out of the sides of hills and happening to cater for audiences of tens of thousands pre-dated the acting styles with their epic sweep, or whether it seemed suitable to house the styles (which could have developed in response to some unknown aesthetic demand) in such a place. When theatre is so ancient, we can only make informed guesses.

The Restoration theatre in England was an intimate theatre, retaining much of the direct contact between actor and audience of the Elizabethan stage. With each rebuilding the stage was moved farther back towards the proscenium, until we are eventually forced to envisage a sort of bas-relief presentation, utilizing a thin strip of the front of the stage which was well lit (the back of the stage was not). The lights were on in the auditorium throughout the

performance: there is no way of extinguishing and re-lighting thousands of candles with any ease. What are the implications of this? The intimacy had been replaced by a need to grab the attention of the audience, which in turn was busy studying the rest of the audience and enjoying a social evening, chatting with friends. Fanny Burney's lurid description of an evening at the opera, in *Cecilia*, convincingly shows that the performers were up against fearful odds. The heroine is most unfashionable in wishing to hear the opera in the first place; when she finally gets into the pit, she cannot hear it for the conversation going on around her. But the final indignation is provided by the behaviour of the gentlemen present.

> But what more even than their talking provoked her, was finding that the moment the act was over, when she cared not if their vociferation had been incessant, one of them called out, 'Come, be quiet, the dance is begun;' and then they were all again silent attention.
>
> (Fanny Burney, 1782, *Cecilia*, vol. 1, book 2, ch. 4.)

By the time the capacity of the auditoria had risen to 3000 the noise must have been a dire enemy. John Philip Kemble once stopped mid-tragedy and announced to the mother of a screaming infant, 'Madam, either the baby goes on or I do.' The plays that survive from this era make it very plain that the word had a hard time: the content of the plays decreases in intellectual interest, and loses ground to the spectacular, and to the bombastic mode of acting. But which came first? Theatrical machinery had been available for many years: Inigo Jones created wonders with it at the early Stuart courts, and Henry Fielding was complaining of it as used in pantomime in the 1740s. It formed one of the main attractions of what was, to him, a senseless entertainment. Addison also inveighed against spectacle — in the opera — in *The Spectator*: the machinery and spectacle of opera did not seem to obey common sense — but then Addison thought that opera itself did not make sense.

Nearly two hundred years later Weedon Grossmith had a part in *The Flood Tide* at Drury Lane, one in a tradition of spectacularly realistic plays. Reading the stage directions for the flood scene itself sent him straight round to the Strand to take out a large insurance policy. His character in the play climbs roofs, swings from gables and trees, is caught up in the swirl of the flood.

This kind of spectacle was, in its own way, realistic. Nowadays we would use film for such effects, and can consider the stage freed to return to basics. But we may also have lost some excitement: the flood scene was an attraction of the kind that Meyerhold would have appreciated. There always seems to be a division in attitudes towards available technologies in theatre: does the use of them trivialize or enlarge the action? Do you deny them as ephemera or embrace them as part of the reality of the age in which you live? One of the most influential changes in theatre came about through technological development: the introduction first of gas and then of electric lighting. All at once the audience could be plunged into darkness, and, since darkness is not conducive to talk, plunged into silence. People in the audience felt themselves to be individuals rather than part of a large crowd, and there was a new intimacy between the individuals and the stage — the entry of a level of fantasy unavailable in bright light. Shaw was all for it, as he thought it guaranteed the audience against self-consciousness. Dürrenmatt denounced it as treacherous, 'for it alone made possible the solemn atmosphere in which our theatres suffocate. The stage became a peep show.' He saw this as the logical outcome of the court theatre with its craving for naturalness. Its true successor has been the cinema, with its ability to do what all stage machinery, finally, could not: simulate reality.

> The movies, then, are nothing more nor less than the democratic form of the court theatre. They intensify our sense of intimacy immeasurably, so much so that the movies easily risk becoming the genuinely pornographic art. For the spectator is forced into being a 'voyeur'.

(Friedrich Dürrenmatt, 1955, 'Problems of the theatre' reprinted in R. Corrigan, ed., 1963 *Theatre in the Twentieth Century*, Grove Press, p. 54.)

Architectural alternatives

A classic question: What is the shape automatically invented by people when they, for instance, gather round an accident? Its answer: They form a circle. Having gone into some of the attributes and attritions of the predominant theatre form in contemporary Europe, it is time we looked at what is probably the oldest of theatre forms: theatre in the round. It does not, by the way, have to be round in shape — ellipses and rectangles are actually more useful. A theatre in the round is one in which the acting area is surrounded by the audience. Stephen Joseph, one of its greatest advocates, surmised its beginnings in primitive society. Feeling a need to express themselves, primitive peoples most probably developed dancing: they used it to explore their relationship with their environment, and to try to influence its behaviour. In exerting will power in this manner, the dance developed further into a form of negotiation with the gods — the dancers taking on the role of priests. Performing in the open air, surrounded informally by their fellows, they bargained for the future. To add to the power of the dance, they gradually enlisted the essential equipment of the actor: masks, costumes, paint. And they used sound. From this grew music, song and language, the latter rapidly becoming the most powerful of the actor's weapons. The drama became formal as control over material surroundings developed into civilization: special days and places became necessary. The drama took place on circular threshing floors, but as it grew in popularity, these were not structured well enough to allow everyone to see. Sloping ground would be an advantage, but it is rare that a natural theatre can be found that fulfils all these conditions; and so the compromise of the amphitheatre arose. Roman circuses were in the round, and there is evidence of medieval theatre in the round in England. Plans attached to the Cornish plays show the use of simultaneous setting on the edge of the circle and both actors and audience using the centre.

Why is theatre in the round interesting to us now? Priestley once said that if beginning again he would write for the round because it left everything to the imagination. Stephen Joseph shows how the level of the actual stage relates to the status of the protagonist *vis-á-vis* the audience. In the old plays on raised stages, kings and heroes looked down on the audience. In modern plays, with protagonists on the same level figuratively with the audience, they should be seen literally on the same level. And they are brought closer by the fact that their background is the audience, human beings who are thus engaged in the responsibility for the action. Seen in this way

> it is just possible to conceive the idea of a theatre that increases our sensitivity to moral responsibility and exercises our little-used power of choice.... To exercise this power of choice, to engage our will power, is an important function of the theatre; for these activities are too much hindered during most of our lives and, since they are an essential part of human nature, we are so far robbed of our humanity. Here in the theatre, it seems to me, we can make some preparation to deal with real problems of existence.

(Stephen Joseph, 1967, *Theatre in the Round*, Barrie & Rockcliff, pp. 121–2.)

The apparently neutral subject of spaces leads straight into a discussion of their function, the impact they have on the community using them: a morality of form, if you like.

Theatre forms lying somewhere between the round and the proscenium arch incorporate different kinds of separation of the audience from the stage. The stage is at one end of the room, the audience at the other. Different arrangements produce differing amounts of contact. The arena or thrust stage juts fairly far out into the audience, as at Chichester; the end stage is a rectangular shape where the stage is simply the other end of the room, as at the Mermaid. Superfluous details have vanished. Many modern theatres are built as complexes, including concert halls and studios.

Others are flexible and can be changed to suit the play. The New London Theatre can even move the seating by revolving it outside the building. Brave new world? C. Curio did it in Rome in about 50 BC, according to Pliny, but he

had two theatres, which turned on pivots. In the morning, back to back, each audience watched the games. Later in the day they would swing to face each other to form an amphitheatre for gladiatorial combats. And there were other variations. So far as I know, the audiences at the New London have not been treated so royally as the Roman populace; and the idea of flexibility loses its charm when contact is lost with the audience, as seems to be the case at the New London.

This kind of bad planning arises from a failure by the architects to find the right starting point. Theatre architects should be conscientious theatre-goers, both as audience and behind stage. They should understand every aspect of the theatre act, all the inter-relationships. Above all, they must experience what it is like to be in the audience. No amount of gadgetry can replace the actor—audience relationship, but if that is once understood, flexibility can be made to serve a useful purpose. Meyerhold wanted theatre to be chameleon, and managed to achieve a new form for each play. Piscator's plans for a Total Theatre were never carried out, unfortunately. Walter Gropius was the architect, and his ideas commenced in the audience.

> The starting point for my design ... was provided by the memory of an unforgettable experience I had had at a Reinhardt production at the Deutches Theater. At a moment of great dramatic tension an actor had suddenly spoken from a box at the back of the stalls. The effect was tremendous. I felt as if I were physically involved in the events being portrayed on the stage. The dividing line between the real and the stage world had suddenly vanished. One was forced into active participation in the drama.... I produced a plan which included all three classic stage forms — the 'apron' stage, the proscenium stage and the arena stage, all in one theatre so that the producer could use whichever one suited him. Film projectors were located all round the sides of the theatre, some pointing at the roof, so that the scenery could be created behind and above the spectators as well, thus giving them the illusion of being totally involved in the drama.
> .(Unpublished letter in the Piscator Archive, Catalogue to the Arts Council exhibition, Erwin Piscator, Political Theatre 1920–1966, n.d., p. 35.)

Off-centre

Fringe theatre is poor theatre. Theatre made out of spaces originally intended for something else, or taking its chances along with other activities. Such spaces really do need flexibility, since much experimentation takes place in fringe groups; and they require economy. A space, a good set of lighting bars to hang the lamps from, and something comfortable to sit on: those are the basics. The old Arts Lab in Drury Lane was one of the most comfortable and interesting of spaces, full of small rooms with mattresses on which you could, if the place was not full, lie down to watch plays (and they did look different from this position). Other theatres have been created out of church halls, which have an unfortunate tendency to remain rather unfriendly as buildings; or take the form of transportable temporary structures, like the Bubble Theatre's plastic bubble, which tours the Greater London area. It can be set up almost anywhere.

And here we are, outside actual buildings, moving towards the street. Political theatre groups perform anywhere, including the street; permanent theatre buildings often act to hamper their work. They take their theatre to their audiences, performing at factory gates, in canteens, in schools, in parks. If you want your work to be seen as in integral part of life, then it must be released from the cage first.

Against these 'poor' theatres (Peter Brook calls them 'rough'), the rich ones stand out more clearly. For some years the Arts Council had a policy called Housing the Arts. It invested in buildings. The National Theatre, although ideas for it predate this policy by decades, epitomizes this trend. The enormous amount of money poured into concrete could have sustained many groups for many years reaching a wider audience. And, as to the actual National as a building, it is not even certain that the spaces in it are the right ones. Grotowski told Kenneth Tynan that the main theatres are far too large: this is an age in need of intimate theatres. But the need for hugeness does not arise from theatrical concerns; it is to do with the monolithic idea of the National as a showplace for the nation. At the time of writing, the Lyttelton is-the only theatre in the complex open. It is an enormous and forbidding black hole, its vertical lines unalleviated by horizontals. The balconies are not visible from the stalls. And from the balcony you have the effect of looking at the stage down the wrong end of a telescope. The overall effect is rather oppressive. It is hoped that various events and activities will take place around the outside of the concrete mass, in an attempt to humanize the place.

Stephen Joseph was once asked what he would consider the most important feature of a National Theatre.

> 'The most important thing is to make it inflammable,' he said, 'so that by the time they realize they've made a mess of the place it can be burned down and they can start again.'

(Quoted by Peter Cheeseman in Judith Cook, 1974, *Director's Theatre*, p. 34.)

The art of midwifery

One of the fascinations of theatre is that it is a collective alliance of all the arts: performing, visual, aural. The potential involved in synthesizing them into a focus having a public confrontation is enormous. It is a philosopher's stone but it must be used with care. If you forget that audience—actor essence, you may well find you have sabotaged your own work.

The director is a recent innovation, the baby of the theatre. But he has become its midwife. Sheridan caused a minor scandal when he insisted on rehearsing *The School for Scandal* when it was first performed in Bath in 1777. The actors felt insulted by his action. While authors still do not often rehearse their plays, people would be astonished if no director appeared for this purpose today. The director has rapidly acquired much power: the power to choose what plays shall be done, by whom, and how. Hebbel described the work of the director as 'to present the necessary in the form of the accidental, that is the whole secret of dramatic style.' A style is discovered for each play: it is never to be put on like an overcoat because it worked last time. But how is the thing to be achieved?

> Between the dramatist's impulse for theatre art and the actual realization of that impulse lie countless mediators, pressing vitally individual impurities into an event that must finally appear whole, inevitable, and

Try, from your own experience, to define what theatre is about or for Need it be about or for anything?

commandingly pure. While the director represents, in a sense, the master mediator, he is also something more: a receding presence, the artist who is felt most when his hand is seen least.

(Gordon Rogoff, 1973, 'The director's eye' *The Drama Review*, vol. 9, no. 3, p. 102.)

How does this mediator work? Firstly, the director must want to do the play; then begins working on it by reading it many times in order to understand how the overall action of the play is served by characters and given circumstances. Research may be needed into historical detail. The idea for a set may appear early on, but should be prevented from becoming fixed. The actual space in which the play is to happen must be examined for potentiai. And the director must have an idea of the relationship the play is to have with the audience. On top of that, knowing how actors work is the most important thing. The old-fashioned authoritarian director who treats actors as puppets and tells them exactly what to do has become intolerable: the actors' creative work is vital to the development of the play, and must be encouraged by every means. Actors and director together create a mutual stage reality which enables them to use the potential of the stage for expressiveness. The director arrives at the first rehearsal with a body of knowledge about the play and some clear insights as to the possible manner of performance. Some directors proceed to talk about the meaning of the play, others do not mention it. The one thing they should not do is say how the play should be performed: this is a sure way of killing the actors' ability to make of themselves a creative journey through the text.

Nobody is interested in working on problems which have already been answered, the 'the butler did it' syndrome.

Creative acts, by director and actors, arise from a quest for meaning and another quest to render the meaning meaningful. The play and the production have rightly been called an unbroken intellectual line. The audience watching a play in which this process has been prevented or short-circuited, coughs, shuffles and knows that something is wrong. They are right. The play has been stillborn, even though it may look, on the surface, perfectly formed.

Improvisation is increasingly used as a rehearsal technique, freeing the performers from preconceived ideas about their parts, and allowing them to develop deeper levels of meaning for them. Above all, it provides help with motivation on stage: each action must have a motive, and the entire play can be broken down from a super-objective into a series of motivations for individual scenes, and beats within scenes. The director can use improvisation in a general sense, or select those games which will help to sort out a particular problem. There are stages when the director needs to be a quiet watcher of the actors' work, without interfering, letting the play find its pace and a sense of totality.

He should know as much as possible about audience expectations since this may prove a vital factor in the presentation of the work. Are they likely to be friendly or hostile to the content before it starts? Do you feel that shock effects will enhance the meaning of the play? Will they grasp the message without explanation? These considerations affect the way that meaning and style are welded on stage. It is, perhaps, this very social aspect of theatre that has made the great directors into great theorists and inventors, as they struggle at one and the same time with the abstract and the concrete in their work.

Pictures, props and principles

The director and the designer work very closely to create the optimum conditions for revealing the meaning of the play and enabling the actors to create. Good design is not décor but structure. As such, the designer must go through some of the processes that the director does in order to create the appropriate setting.

Scenography has been suggested as the best word to cover the multitude of things that design in theatre involves: it is the art of translation to a fine degree. Making the subjective objective involves two- and three-dimensional structures, costume, props, lighting. It is a plastic language, according to Josef Svoboda, and

> Fundamentally, it is not a question of the accidental composition of elements or even relationships, but the creation of dramatic plans which can be changed in the course of the action, appearing and disappearing as required by the dramatic tension.

(R. Hainaux, ed., 1973, *Stage Design throughout the World since 1960*, Harrap, p. 12.)

It is the relation between movement and stasis that creates plasticity. Gordon Craig and Stanislavsky were agreed on the power of movement to express invisible things, inner realities. We recognize easily the association between inner life and the body, but need to be reminded that all bodily action is through space. Stage design must be sensitive to the actor as physical entity,

to the possibility of dialogue between different sorts of space on stage, since design cannot exist on stage until it is in use. It should have no independent meaning. But it should contribute to the overall dramatic style and deal with the realities of the particular theatre at the same time. Innovations in scenography have come from the directors struggling to put new *content* on stage and finding that new *forms* are necessary for this.

The design of costumes or props must also help in the development of images which aid the expressiveness of the play. They must be in the style of the play; they use light and colour; they should express character in the light of the particular way the play is being interpreted, and they should feel right to the actor. They are a harmonic part of the overall vision. The designer needs everything and nothing when approaching a play. As the Swedish designer, Carl-Johan Ström says,

> My theatrical colleagues and I always say that starting work on a new production ought to be the same thing as embarking on a new profession. Methods, materials and technique should be strictly adapted to the character of the enterprise.
> (*Stage Design throughout the World since 1960*, p. 12.)

Like the director, the designer must also remember that the actor may create, demand exactly the right object, find such things for himself. Actors use props for specific purposes and consequently have very clear ideas on them. For instance, in the afterpiece to *The Fire Raisers*, the maid has to bring the Devil his head waiter's wig, before he returns to earth. The scene is comic overall, but we, the performers, felt its menace should be made clearer. Initially we suggested a skull for the wig block, and a mirror as a tray. This developed into using a severed head and the mirror; and very gruesome the image was. The mirror held up, towards the audience, was to remind them for a few seconds that the play was about them, and the severed head showed the result of their actions. The image produced by the two objects was a reminder of the theme of the play as against the whimsy enveloping the afterpiece.

If you are planning to experiment with design outside an actual production, you are free of some of the constraints; or, rather, they are there in the abstract. Ideally, your ideal vision should contain the possibility of life, which entails considering audience, actors and space. However, it is very good practice to investigate the possibilities for, say, one play: how to express its meaning using sound alone, or light alone, or constructions, or colour, or extraordinary costumes.... It is a way of building up a repertoire of ideas on how to have ideas about visual aspects of the play.

Theatrical things and people in life
Keep a record of these. What makes them theatrical? Ritual, participation in an event, the scale of an event, somebody's everyday gestures that seem larger than necessary? Could you call them theatre, as well as theatrical? If not, what is the difference?

3 WHY IS THE AUDIENCE THERE?

Audiences are there to see plays; and, leaving aside the rituals surrounding theatre, the play contains the major clues to the activity of theatre-going and the importance on theatre as an institution.

Back numbers and advance parties: The plays

The attempt to analyse plays in the abstract usually falls back on a discussion of genres: the tragic, the comic, and so on. These are often presented as absolute and ahistorical modes. However, it is clear that there are recognizable periods which have been especially amenable to the tragic mode rather than the comic, and vice versa. Raymond Williams's *Modern Tragedy* is one of the best examinations of this phenomenon. Williams comes to the conclusion that

> Important tragedy seems to occur, neither in periods of real stability, nor in periods of open and decisive conflict. Its most common historical setting is the period preceding the substantial breakdown and transformation of an important culture. Its condition is the real tension between old and new: between received beliefs, embodied in institutions and responses, and new and vividly experienced contradictions and possibilities.
> (Raymond Williams, 1966, *Modern Tragedy*, Chatto & Windus, p. 54.)

Even the most absolute of categories exists within history.

When Aristotle defined the drama, in *The Poetics*, Greek tragedy was going through a particularly purple patch, and his definitions were derived from actual theatre practice at that time. The critics who later turned his findings into the Rules of Drama, ignoring the derivation, were responsible for taming otherwise forceful statements by forcing them through an unnatural practice. The 'felt life' of the play vanished under adherence to the rules. Aesthetic theories are important for our comprehension of particular phases of drama, and for examining the potential of the medium. But, however abstract they are, their derivation is always the art work.

A law and a theory are not identical. The tendency of the theorist to lay down the law is, luckily, undermined by the tendency of dramatists to flout it: in itself a factor in their creativity. The consciousness of the great dramatists seems to be in advance of their contemporaries. Of course, many of these dramatists also turned critic: practice often produces the best theory. Drama critics (in the literary sense) who deny that a play must be understood in relation to performance are denying the intentions of the author.

And drama critics (in the newspaper sense) who have no knowledge of theatre history are equally guilty of creating a vacuum for understanding. Theory and practice are always linked.

Meaning and matter: Theory

To write a play is to create a mode of articulation for meaning. The articulation and the meaning are dialectically connected so as to utilize the tensions to produce, finally, a sign: the play.

If we examine a play in the light of this semiological approach, we may get close to the creative process and come to grips with the reasons for the depth of the experience of good drama.

First of all, as a piece of *literature*, the play signifies a command of knowledge, an ability to abstract the particular from the general, and the ability to utilize language — the most human of human constructs. In this very fact there is a pointer to the common critical stress of theatre as an *educational* structure. Since most plays deal with people (known as characters) the knowledge

Can a play 'claim' anything?

inhering in the play must refer to the things which separate people from animals and inanimate objects. In this we see a parallelism with *humanitarian concepts*; the more we understand about the behaviour and ideals of people, the more likely we are to make a humane social order.

Since the structural presentation — the articulation — of these levels of theatre coincides with the creation of a highly determined sign (the play), to which, however, there may be a variety of responses (individual reactions that go to make up a collective reaction), a very powerful order of being attaches to the play. An order of being in which, however briefly, diverse people come together in an agreement over a sign which relates to the actual and possible behaviour of human beings, as revealed through the collective effort of writing, producing and assisting at the play.

Consciously or unconsciously the writer is aware of the sign systems of theatre and uses them in formulating the articulation. These systems are not just the conventions, but also the behaviour of the audience and common knowledge brought to any event. The systems allow for communication, but if the playwright is not sufficiently aware of them, the meaning of the play may be distorted. If this makes writing plays sound like a wrestling match, well, maybe it is rather like that. Brecht summed up the dangers of not understanding the life led by sign systems and conventions.

> The necessity to stage the new drama correctly — which matters more for the theatre's sake than for the drama's — is modified by the fact that the theatre can stage anything: it theatres it all down.
> (Bertolt Brecht, Notes to *The Threepenny Opera*.)

Being aware of the sign systems and the underlying economic or social motivation for them makes for a leaping-off point for intuitive, creative work which will not be distorted, but encouraged to find its own mode. The playwright's intention to create meaning should be the subsoil for all the theatrical growth that accrues thereafter.

The play that claims to have no intrinsic meaning is a lie. It has been demonstrated that, for instance, the majority of West End plays and the multitude of copies used in amateur drama festivals, indeed much of the output of both television and radio drama (especially serials) are suffused with reassurance about the *status quo*. Whatever else happens during the play, we can rest assured (i.e. remain passive) that things right themselves in the end and that there is a stable 'natural' order: human beings are always the same. The message of passivity is precisely what Brecht described as 'the general drug traffic conducted by bourgeois show business.' This statement is not 'against entertainment', but entertainment does not exist *as such* any more than does any other cultural construct. People can be 'taken out of themselves' equally well by 'savage insights'. But they return to themselves at different places. Back to square one? Or make some progress?

Meaning and articulation: Theory in relation to practice

It was Howard Brenton who cited 'savage insights' as the object of theatre. As the most public of art forms, theatre must tell the truth so strongly that it will 'act like a bush-fire, smouldering into public consciousness.' But it has to do this in an appropriate way. In an age that thas produced real tragedies on such a vast scale (two world wars, for a start) tragedy on stage seems to have changed. Martin Esslin argues that it exists in the theatre of the absurd, with the menace arising from the portraits of meaninglessness, non-communication and so on. Brenton would agree with the critics who disagree that this is tragedy with the values Esslin attaches to it: they claim that it, too, says ultimately, 'This is how it is and nothing can be done,' and it therefore is just another version of reassurance. One can go to the theatre, be harrowed, and come home feeling that one has done something by living through the experience. Brenton wants things to happen as a result of the consciousness produced by the play, but the very seriousness of his intention has made him examine how to deal with it. He concludes:

> It's very profound, comic writing; it's the one common link between performance and audience. In the past, you could say there were other things that would bind performers and audience together — like religion. . . . But the only thing that binds us together today is profound unease, and laughter is the language of that unease.
> (Howard Brenton, 1975, 'Petrol bombs through the proscenium arch', interview in *Theatre Quarterly*, vol. 5, no. 17, p. 6.)

Many contemporary playwrights employ a mixture of genres within one play, thus producing additional levels of complexity to match that of reality, as the interweaving of sign systems gives depth to the experience.

The greatest writers on this relationship between theory and practice, between intention and articulation, are those who are conscious of the need to understand the relationship. They want to change it: this involves analysing it. The writers who have become classic writers in the modern period have all initiated new relationships and written about them. Pirandello, exploring philosophical and psychological idea, transformed the potential of stage reality. Brecht's theory of alienation, deriving from the intention to make the theatre, as Piscator would have put it, a parliament, where people would understand reality, not sink into feelings, theorizes about every aspect of theatre. And uses everything available to produce the desired effect. Thus he joins Piscator in advanced uses of technology in the theatre, at the same time as he develops new theories about acting. The theatre should be at one and the same time a forum for political ideas, and fun. This requires players who 'have acquired a contradictory spirit, independence of judgement, and social imagination' and who know that thinking is 'a way of behaving, and behaving socially at that. It's something the body takes part in, with all its senses.' Theatre should demonstrate the possibility of change.

The whole theatre act is a social one — a microcosm of the process of social creation. The collective transformation that takes place during rehearsals is felt by the audience as a positive offering of possibilities. The audience are part of the long journey and process of analysis, emotional response, and decision making: if the play is trivial in intention, all this work is betrayed by being frittered.

The show so far

The show so far has admittedly been a skating session across the top layer of an enormous body of work and theory. I can only hope to open up the discussion: the book list at the end of the unit should enable you to follow up aspects of theatre that you find particularly interesting. For me, the interesting thing in talking about theatre is its public nature, its various functions in various societies. Even the synthesizing artistic aspects depend on this kind of interest, if design in theatre is to have any meaning for the audience.

Theatre is an enormous risk taken in public, the one art form where artists and public confront each other in real physical space, where there is, in a sense, no escape. They deal with ideas together as well as sharing enjoyment. Theatre's ability to render the idea concrete, to make the image produce thought, its ability to add to knowledge, has always been acknowledged, even if only in the negative form of censorship. After all, it was Fielding's *success* in ridiculing Walpole which led the latter to introduce the Licensing Act of 1737.

Is there a doctor in the house?

You should be comparing your own experience of theatre with the ideas I have been discussing, trying them out, if you like. But you do not have to like them for the methods of approaching the subject to be of value. Then there is also the more general problem of criticism. Criticism of performances ought to be able to help the theatre workers see what more could be achieved. Unfortunately, most newspaper criticism is so ill-informed and so self-limiting as to be useless. Hardly any critic asks the important question, Was the play worth writing, worth the effort lavished on it? Critics must be able to distinguish between text, direction, and acting, but do not achieve this very often. Still caught up in the star system, they pay far too much attention to the acting at the expense of the rest of the work.

The show so far is only *part* of the show. I have examined the conventional theatre in detail because it allows a discussion of all the separate elements that make up theatre. In itself, it sometimes is revitalized. But used in other theatre situations, these elements can be very different. There is infinitely more to theatre than the ideal embodied in the National complex on the South Bank.

> Can you see any difference between drama and theatre?
> Can you see any difference between spectacle and an art show?
> When does a play become a play?

4 WILL THE REAL NATIONAL THEATRE PLEASE STAND UP?

Alternatives

'The fringe' was once a term referring to the non-establishment side of the Edinburgh Festival. It generally produced experimental work. Some of this definition still clings to the fringe as it refers to the body of small theatres, mostly in London but with outposts throughout the country. It does still have a strong sense of experimentation, although, as in conventional theatre, shows can be boring, or superficial. When it started, it was a protest against many of the conditions of work in establishment theatres. Professional theatre can take up an actor's life in the churning out of rubbish or leave him out of work for such long periods that the arrival of a part, even if in a play with which he disagrees, is heaven-sent and no quarrel with the play seems possible. It was also partly a desire to reach different, wider audiences, and the desire to experiment with the very languages of theatre.

From the fringe (as from off-off Broadway in New York) there emerged a large number of new playwrights and acting groups, working very often on a collective basis, experimenting with the material of theatre. The effects of their work can even be seen now in conventional theatre: the dominant cultural form always does take up new ideas which can be absorbed. The ideas it rejects are the ones involving structural change: the collective rather than the hierarchical organization, for instance, where the role of the director is merged among the actors, and the choosing of plays is agreed on by all.

Many groups lived collectively, to underline the point about the relationship between theory and practice. The Living Theatre was the largest example of this, and, with its improvisational techniques and its montage/collage manner of developing plays through the association of themes, was very influential. Living Theatre, in fact, was very caught up with the idea of anarchy as creative, and the revolution that was to follow from this. Its good performances were very impressive. The other aspect of their work which captured popular myth-making was that of participation, physical involvement with the audience. There were very strange sides to this: very often the audience would be frustrated by being encouraged to participate and then not being allowed to do so: an authoritarian anomaly amid the anarchism and the genuinely resonant associations evoked by their collage pieces.

Other groups worked closely with playwrights, either on individual plays or continuously. Portable and Freehold and their playwrights developed each other's ways of expressing ideas through the common development within the group. Most groups worked very hard on the non-verbal aspects of theatre, a side of the experimental work that led off more recently into what is called ritual theatre. (This is something of which I am personally very suspicious; it seems to me a form of escapism, to deny the value of language and to attempt to set up spurious underlying meanings when there are so many real ones to work with.)

One of the few groups from the fringe which still works as it did, and which is possibly the most original in its attack on traditional theatre, is the People Show. Their shows never have names, just the number of the show they have reached. The shows are part fixed, part improvised around an assemblage of images gradually brought together, and which always resemble some form of fertile junkyard. The meaning of the show is what the audience discovers in it; some of this is shared, since audiences do share cultural assumptions, and ideas about beauty; others are individual, as certain images set up an individual resonance. It is often slightly threatening to be at a People Show, and much of its interest lies in the fact that anything can happen. The content of the shows (and they are definitely not happenings, they are far more formal) is an anti-aesthetic assault, at base.

What has happened to the fringe? The main thing that happened was that it failed to attract a really different audience. There were perhaps more young people who had not previously begun to attend theatre: but they were strictly middle class, the same basic audience that attends Royal Shakespeare Company plays. Added to this was the failure of the May 1968 uprising in Paris, which felled in its wake many people's hopes that collective creative action could bring change of any lasting and large sort. Working in the fringe began to seem self-indulgent. People who were really interested in reaching new audiences left, to join the growing number of community theatres. The people staying behind were somewhat trapped in a semi-institutionalized situation, where actors work for nothing much of the time in order to ameliorate being out of work, and occasionally because the play really interests them. It is not all bad: now and then there are lights flashing in the gloom. And although one feels that the *main* action has moved on, both for democratic reasons and for the sake of those lights — the experimental work that still emerges in the fringe — subsidies to the fringe should be increased to recognize its part in contemporary theatre.

Can a rehearsal
be a great
performance?
What is the
difference between a
good play and a bad
one?
What does 'tragic'
mean to you?
And 'tragedy'?

Community theatre

Community theatre covers a number of areas, all of which share a certain amount of common background in the idea of people's theatre.

People's theatre leans on the main stream of popular entertainment forms, including circuses, processions and pop concerts. Far from needing to create ritual theatre, in fact, the generation that was in its early twenties in the 1960s already has its own ritual theatre — the rock festival. Woodstock demonstrated the common bonds between that generation and strengthened them through the music that internationalized that aspect of culture. Altamont demonstrated the other extreme — the violence underlying the 'peace and love' movement, the violence which had provoked a need for it but which could not hope to cure it. Rock festivals and big rock concerts are very theatrical; after all, some of the fans are so far from the stage that they cannot see the faces of the singers. Light shows and machinery — spectacle — are provided in compensation.

The other common background is the theatre of the working class, covering a variety of forms from the Victorian penny gaff to the self-styled workers' theatre movements of the 1920s and 1930s in Europe and the United States of America. When you examine these forms, you find that the workers took theatre far more seriously than the prevalent idea that only entertainment is suitable for them, will allow. Our contemporary picture of music hall is a one-sided distortion of the actual content in its heyday. That sentimental picture of a historical variety show falls apart when you confront the songs: they were political, critical, satirical. Of course, there were some sentimental pieces, but modern television renderings simply censor out the songs ridiculing the royal family, protesting against jingoism, giving vivid and angry descriptions of working-class life. And the music hall included sketches, which grew into plays eventually. Giving evidence to the Select Committee on Theatre and Places of Entertainment in 1892, managers pointed out that profits rose whenever sketches were shown, and a representative of the London United Workmen's Committee affirmed that 'a gradual and continuous improvement in the character of the entertainment provided by the managers' had been noticed and, at the date of the inquiry, 'music halls have reached a very high state of morality, and can compare very favourably with the theatres'. Earlier in the century, two shows were offered at the theatres: Shakespeare first, and then more 'popular' forms. It has been pointed out that working-class people, whose jobs started earlier in the day and finished earlier than those of middle class clerks in offices, came to the Shakespeare. Attitudes die hard. Who knows what summer variety on the pier might offer if there were not the common notion that working people neither care for nor understand serious theatre?

The working-class theatre of the earlier twentieth century included documentary and the kind of content that later became known as kitchen sink. It created the living newspaper, a technique first used by the Federal Theatre Project in New York and paying for a complete staff of journalists. This was introduced into the United Kingdom by Unity Theatre, and Theatre Union (in Manchester), where Ewan MacColl wrote *Last Edition*. This last dealt with the entire Munich period and was constantly updated. It was closed by the police about three weeks before war broke out, on the grounds of causing a public disturbance. Using multiple levels of staging, local, national and international events could be linked simultaneously. The most recent group to do living newspapers is Combine, who have a less high-powered version.

A varied group of theatre activities can be summed up under the heading 'social theatre'. This includes theatre as therapy, much educational theatre, taking culture to the masses, and giving people the experience of creativity, self-confidence and awareness. Many groups include some of these ideas alongside their more strictly aesthetic offerings: Phantom Captain is an example of this, offering work on video, encounter sessions, publications and environmental theatre which explores 'the hinterland between "theatre" and "real life"'.

Theatre in education has a span of possibilities, but is caught up very often in the trap of the expectation of finished products, and ceasing to be an enjoyable and spontaneous event amid the very ordered lives of children at school.

'Political theatre' should perhaps be called 'overtly' or 'consciously political theatre', since it can be argued that all theatre is political. These groups come together in a decision to provide theatre which will move people towards political consciousness or action. Sometimes they provide support for a political action, demonstrate solidarity, raise money, document particular events, and expose injustice or oppression.

Within this spectrum are such groups as El Teatro Campesino, which was created specifically to recruit Mexican American farm workers into the union. Its work built from the basic short sketch which made a point, to plays showing the relationship between the struggles of the farmworkers and the oppression of people in the third world. From the start the theatre has been seen as part of the culture and provides cultural centres. From one group originally, a large movement has grown.

In the United Kingdom most people would think of Red Ladder as the typical political group. Red Ladder started as a small agit-prop group in response to a request to present the arguments of a struggle over housing. The company lives and works together, and recently moved from London to Leeds in order to be closer to the hub of their work. They work very closely with the Labour Movement, deciding on new plays according to the needs of the movement, and creating them collectively. They now see the agit-prop side of their work as having limited uses and its influence as very contradictory. The over-simplification of ideas which is necessary for a ten-minute presentation of a large subject also distorts the political content, especially in rendering the workings of the system in the form of individuals. Moreover, the stress of agit-prop as *the* socialist theatre form leads to inverted formalism, a kind of simplistic expressionism. Working-class theatre needs everything it can use, selected carefully. And it should ask questions, not answer them. Like most political theatre groups, Red Ladder perform where they are needed, taking the play to the audience. And it is of the essence in their work that each play is followed by a discussion of considerable length.

The other fairly well-known political theatre group is 7:84. The title refers to the fact that 7 per cent of the population of the United Kingdom own 84 per cent of the land. There are two companies, one in Scotland, the other in England. Their work in Scotland is closely related to the history and current development of the country, focusing on the problems caused by capitalism over the years, and, now, those being created by the North Sea oil boom. In England the plays are rather more general. John McGrath writes the plays, although collective work provides much of the materials for his writing. The plays have the unusual quality of combining highly defined characters in realistic settings with the real effects of politics, and all this, very often, within the framework of a genuine entertainment, making good use of music.

The influence of the rock era can be felt in the work of Cartoon Archetypical Slogan Theatre (CAST), whose shows also utilize Goon Show tactics of quick cutting, and the juxtaposition of ideas as images. The overall element of entertainment is a structural part of their work, not something tagged on. It comes from their understanding of their audience and their own vision of what they are doing. When you perform to people who do not go to theatre, and may even not like it — and they are in an echoing church hall or noisy

Consider any aspect
that comes to mind,
to do with the stage
or with reality.
Do the same with
'comedy' and
'comic'.
How do you think
the theatre/drama
and reality aspects
of these words relate
to each other? Do
you think the
relationships are
sensible? What
about the word
'realism'?

canteen — it is essential to grab their attention and, since there is no need for political theatre to be boring, entertain them. The idea should be to plant some ideas which may come to fruition years later. The one thing that CAST regard as unnecessary is to teach, to use the occasion as an illustrated lecture. This mode of work assumes that the worker understands nothing of his or her own oppression. CAST feel that the factory worker knows more about oppression than most theatre groups do: the task of the theatrical work is therefore agitational and builds on the knowledge of the audience. The result is a series of dynamic images, in which style and politics are inseparable. Any excess of

style for its own sake would be avant-gardism, ignoring the political necessities; and politics proferred almost raw, as in basic agit-prop, while suitable in Russia in order to demonstrate to illiterate peasants what had happened in the Revolution, is an anomaly in contemporary Britain.

Other political groups are based on certain areas of experience: Gay Sweatshop and the Women's Theatre Group, for instance. Yet others are more closely associated with a locality, attempting, as the Half Moon Theatre does in Whitechapel, to make political theatre work for a particular community. Effective political theatre should lead the way to revolutionary theatre, During the Long March, Chinese revolutionary theatre went into peasant areas and persuaded the people there that they should not accept the Japanese invasion, but should fight against it. It used a combination of melodrama and

Try to evaluate a day
in your life by
assigning these
labels to events in it:
for example, you
make breakfast for
your mother who is
visiting and it burns.
Tragic? Tragi-comic?
You face up to a
crisis at work.
Realism? Absurd?
Do this project in
detail. All these
rememberings and
evaluations are
valuable when it
comes to writing, or
creating in theatre,
or criticism. Some
will provide ideas,
images, new ways of
dealing with
ideas. . . .

information. Nowadays it incorporates every variety of traditional theatre, dance and ballad form. Phenomenal numbers of people are involved as performers: in 1975 almost fifty million people were doing amateur theatricals: they were working in schools, factories, on communes.

Theatre in revolutionary Russia took up an idea from the 1789 Revolution in France, and re-enacted — with mass participation — the great events of the Revolution. These enactments, having the character of festivals, involved over ten thousand people at a time.

Talking of 1789, one of the most effective pieces of political theatre has been the Théâtre du Soleil's *1789*. This was developed collectively under the inspiration of Mnouchkine, who insists that the events of 1968 were the crucial turning point in their understanding and questioning of what culture consists of. This radicalization of their ideas was a major factor in their achievement of the fairground/festival/multi-level play. The content of the play — the difference between 'historical truth' and its meaning for individual people — was reflected in the style: the audience watched simultaneously the people discovering disrespect for the ruling classes, and the performance being liberated from conventional dramatic modes.

Improvisational theatre implies a liberation for the participants — at its most extreme this is used in psychodrama to free mental patients from their rigid self-defence systems. It is the basis for all community theatre, since so much of this is built up from ideas, rather than from scripts, and seeks to find new ways of relating to the text and the audience. Improvisational techniques are particularly good for setting and solving problems.

The most radical form of improvisational theatre that I have seen is that of Word and Action (Dorset). They use a form called 'instant theatre', which is exactly what it is. Nothing is worked out in advance. They always work in the round, to involve people fully. Everyone in the audience creates the play, starting from the first word suggested. Every word has to be included in the play, and stories can sometimes become very surrealistic as the audience tests out how far the actors are prepared to go in this acceptance technique. Once it is clear that everything will be included, trust develops and invention lifts off. One of the company acts as a questioner to gather the words, to précis them at various stages, and to cut the scenes so that they do not go over what has been said so far. Instant theatre is a form that aims specifically at releasing the potential for creativity that all people have, without using any psychological jargon. Word and Action also have a writing service, for much the same purpose. Their work centres on the experience of language.

Documentary theatre serves a number of purposes. For Peter Weiss it is a technique of writing conventional plays, for the working-class theatre it demonstrates some aspects of life. But perhaps the most interesting variety is that of the Victoria Theatre at Stoke on Trent. It has been used there as a way of linking the theatre to the community, by investigating and presenting local history. Their play about the North Staffordshire Railway, *The Knotty*, was one of the most exciting pieces of theatre I ever witnessed — and I do not come from Staffordshire. It indicates a fact about theatre: theatre built from the real contact with a community gains in every way from this. The sharpness of detail and truth to life become so vivid that the plays become more universal as a result of being particular.

Happenings and events

Creators of happenings and events aim to expose an unwitting audience to the impact of their environment, to make them see old and worn things in a new way, to lead them to be active or creative when they are least expecting it. Some events make political points. Others are related only to the inner thoughts of the participants. They are plays where everyone becomes a performer, or statements which serve as a kind of living visual art, to shock the

37

Consider the
relationship between
theatre and travel:
the experience of
travel yields
particular things, and
some of them share
with the experience
of theatre.

watcher out of preconceived ideas. It is interesting that many of the original happening artists started as painters, and their work led into a more dynamic form.

The happening has also developed into the base for mixed-media events, and these in turn move in many directions. The Welfare State began as a pop group with artistic leanings and a connection with Albert Hunt's political group at Bradford Art School. It then became an anarchic form of street theatre, much influenced by the work of Bread and Puppet Theatre in the United States of America. But they also worked with the jazz composer, Mike Westbrook to produce epics involving everything from ritual to technologically overwhelming mixed-media events. Some of the ceremonies they create last for months.

Finally, it must be noted that much of the work of community/people's/happening theatre is a response to the degeneration in the quality of life in

mass society. The mass media especially are seen to epitomize the killing of individual response and its replacement with stereotyped images and loss of contact with reality. It is in an attempt to demystify the power of the television especially that many community groups have turned to video: the media must become part of the weaponry.

What does theatre share with games?
With children's play?
With sport?
Make a chart to show what aspects they share, and which aspects are most important to each. Is there anything that they all, absolutely, share? Or are there simply variations?
Consider what other experiences generally (excluding travel) are closest to theatre at its strongest. Does your list include personal experiences? public ones?

5 ACTION

Improvisation

How does improvisation relate to the rest of the unit? Its importance to theatre as a whole must be comprehended. Improvisation is the source of all acting, and, in more psychologicql terms, the key to satisfactory existence: the ability to make decisions, to do things, to create from what is available and what is imagined, to change and progress. It can be used by actors and directors for rehearsal purposes, or for training purposes. It can be used in itself to produce improvisational theatre, where everything is invented in front of the audience, or where the audience does the invention. It can be used for psychodrama in encounter groups and mental hospitals. It can be a base for good street theatre, in building up the ability to react swiftly to new situations.

There is a formula which sums up the secret behind improvisational technique, which keeps improvisation open-ended, and which will become clearer as this section goes on. The formula is

$$WHAT + WHY = HOW$$

I recognize that improvisation is not an easy thing to launch yourself into, and it may prove rather difficult for people who have never tried it to make the extensive use of the games that is possible. However, this is a hazard of teaching at a distance, and I hope that you will have the courage to experiment with the games and discover something of what they offer.

Exercises

Before going on to the improvisational games and warm-ups, it is important that you are relaxed. Relaxing exercises should be used for this, since bodily tensions can stand in the way of imaginative release. All the dance work suggested by Stephanie Roberts in her broadcast notes to 'Anyone Can Dance' can be used for this purpose, and many of them will help in building group understanding in a physical way. I am including some here, as alternatives.

Do you know what it feels like to be completely relaxed? If you have forgotten the sensation, as people do in a tense world, try to find it by doing the following:

Lie on the floor on your back with your arms by your sides. Try to feel yourself as a dead weight. If you have someone to help, it will be easier. Your friend should pick up a limb, say an arm, and then drop it. (Do not do relaxing exercises on a concrete floor, by the way.) The arm should fall back as if dead, completely limp, without your being in control of it at all. When you have finally let go the control of that arm, try other limbs, until you can create the sensation by the mental effort of ceasing to control. If you do this on your own, it is possible to experience dead weight by sitting and just using your arms for the lifting and dropping part.

Remember before you go any further that the exercises should all be done several times, and that when you have finished them, you should rest, on the floor, for at least five minutes before getting up to do anything else. Your breathing will have become very deep and you can get dizzy if you forget to rest. Resting also serves a more aesthetic purpose in allowing you to create a silence from which to work.

Lie on your back on the floor. Tense up one part of your body. Start with a toe, or a foot. Then relax it. Work in this way, concentrating on different parts of your body, so that you can discover how your body responds as an instrument, which parts need attention because they are stiff, how muscles you are ignoring come into play to help balance the one you are tensing.

There seems to be a gap between sections 4 and 5. It is the gap between 'me' and 'I', between learning *about* and learning *through*.

To the series of improvisational exercises, I could add one more. It is a very beautiful one from a Japanese composer, Takehisa Kosugi, and is called *Anima 7*. It consists of any simple action performed *as slowly as possible*. How complex a 'simple action' becomes! When performed by a group of people it is unforgettable, and it is an exercise that one can return to again and again with benefit.

Lie on the floor. Gradually, without using your elbows to help, lift your head and move to a sitting position. Then lean over towards your feet. Stretch as far as you can go. Roll back, again without using the arms.

Stand up, with arms by sides. Lean from the waist down to the right, then return to the upright position. Repeat to the left, forwards and backwards. Lean as far as you can. Remember to stand with your feet slightly apart.

Stand up. Roll down so that you are bent over. Try to feel each vertebra curling, one after the other. Your head will come over first, the rest more gradually. When you are curled down, swing your arms gently from side to side. They should feel very heavy. Then uncurl, vertebra by vertebra until you are upright.

Keep your hands out in front of you so that you can see them, and move them in as many ways as possible. Find out what the physical positions express for you. Make your hands angry, sorrowful, pleased, etc. Change rapidly from one to another.

As a last exercise, think of a large, heavy, unwieldy object which needs to be pushed, pulled, or dealt with in some way that involves the entire body. Then push or pull the imaginary object for a while. A car being pushed uphill, an umbrella that has blown inside out while you try to fight the wind while climbing uphill.... Every muscle should be involved in the exercise. You will be pulling against yourself at the same time as working on the object, otherwise you would fall over. When you come to relax, you should feel as if you have actually been doing the imaginary thing.

Acting games

Why games? There is a reason for using this word. Improvisation depends on trust among the participants. It is necessary to avoid 'being personal' or making judgements on each other's work. But you must have a framework for discussing it. You can eradicate the whole approval/disapproval syndrome by

using games. Games have rules. At the end of the improvisation the assessment is carried out in terms of 'Did they follow the rules or not?' Viola Spolin emphasizes the need to create personal freedom in order to create inventiveness: judgement can kill this. We are all graded again and again by other people as we go through life; improvisation should avoid this entirely and create an atmosphere where experiment can take place in sympathetic surroundings.

Improvisation should release the ability to respond as a total person to the world, to explore the environment in physical and mental ways, to behave spontaneously. All of this is natural ground for therapy, of course, but I would like to emphasize that the games are here for a different purpose. Do not indulge in self-analysis. I cannot prevent you from doing this, but that is not the aim of this part of the unit.

Also remember that a week is an infinitesimal time to spend on improvisational work. You will make only limited progress: do not expect miracles, just try the games.

Another point: it is paradoxical to be writing about improvisation since the experience is the key part of it, and any giving of reasons for the games will cut across your ability to experience the purpose of the games for yourself. There is nothing I can do about this, but note that when my notes seem reticent about purpose, it is a deliberate attempt to try not to box in what you may be able to create. Trust the games to take you somewhere. Individuals add their own ingredients to the game anyway, and so I could not define exactly what you should feel at the end of one.

If you are on your own, look through to see which games you think are amenable to being done by one person. Your own circumstances will decide this.

Writing and improvisation

Improvisation can be used to achieve a written script. Imagine the scene of the play and the characters and use the games to create realities with them.

The games

1   One person of the group should get up and walk round in a circle in front of the others. Each person should do this separately, one after the other. What

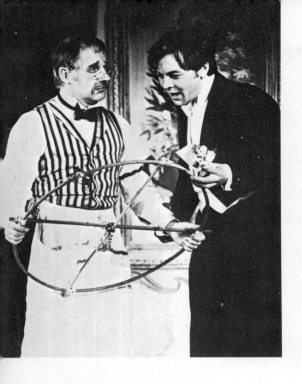

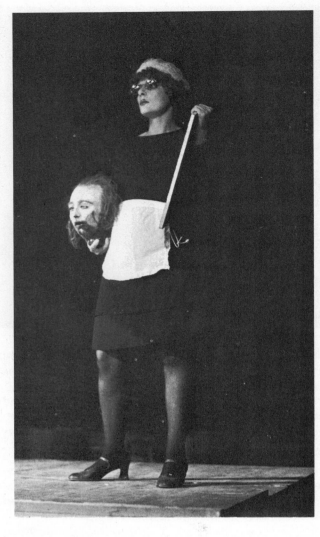

does it feel like? What does it look like? Try again, but this time give the walker something to do, count roses on the wallpaper or something. What does it feel and look like this time?

There will be a difference. On the first time, you will feel awkward and look funny; on the second time, you will feel natural and look natural. This is because you have something to *do* on the second occasion.

From now on, these games should be played by two people at a time, unless otherwise specified. To prevent yourselves writing dialogue in advance, take no more than two minutes to prepare what you are going to do. Ideally, you should be able to reduce this to thirty seconds (after some months). The improvisation itself should be aimed at taking two minutes, also. If it is interesting, let it carry on. But each game is a problem-solving session, and when the problem is solved, the improvisation is finished. After it is over, discuss whether the rules were kept or not, and what might be done to keep them better.

2   *Verbs.* Choose two verbs and work out an improvisation around them. Try this a number of times, to find which verbs work best. The audience is to say at the end which verbs you were doing. For instance, Fred chooses 'to sleep' and Jane 'to pour the tea'. Scene: Jane enters with tea, pours it, gives it to Fred, who wakes and drinks it.

Analysis: What verb was Fred doing? Audience: 'to snore', 'to not want to get up', etc., anything but 'to sleep'. And Jane? Unanimous response: 'to wake Fred up'. The audience gets it wrong because the verbs are useless. Verbs

need to be motivating. They could have had a fine scene with 'to annoy' and 'to persuade', for instance. You must work with verbs to find which ones do work. Also, do not try at first to work with 'to want to...' or 'to try to...' verbs. Try these later on. At the moment we are looking for verbs that allow for contact between the people of the scene. 'To want to...' etc. rely on being able to impede this process.

Verbs should generate real action in the scene, rather than activity.

Verbs, however, are not enough. They are the backbone of the games. But to them must be added the things that build up character and time and place and weather.... But as you go on to deal with these, the verb is still the first thing you choose, and the first thing the audience talks about.

3 Improvise a scene in order to show (not tell) the audience *where* you are through the use of objects. The audience must say where you are at the end.

4 Improvise a scene that shows where you were before you entered.

5 Improvise a scene showing where you are going when you leave. I say show, not tell; if you enter and say, 'I'm just off to the pub, dear,' the game is over before it has started. It relies on the place not being spoken in this way.

6 Improvise a scene in which the way you use objects shows *who* you are.

7 Improvise a scene in which the way you use the place you are in (i.e. the imaginary place) shows *who* you are.

8 Improvise a scene to show what time it is.

9   Improvise a scene showing what the weather is like.

10   Improvise a scene showing *what* you are (job, profession, role in life, etc.)

11   Improvise a scene showing a very large environment.

12   Improvise a scene showing a trapped environment.

Do not forget the questions and answers at the end of each scene. You will find that certain problems come up, such as, 'How were we to know that Fred was a defrocked priest, when so much else was going on?' You will find that the verbs you choose will play a vital role in making clear what is happening, without giving it away. The wrong verbs will obscure the issue. Try to invent new problems for scene-making in order to answer the ones that have arisen. Fred's priest might have been helped by adding 'Where had he come from?' to the things he had to do in the scene, for instance.

13   Improvise your scene so that you have two verbs, one as usual, 'to do ... (whatever it is), the other, 'in order to....' This second verb is known as the super-objective, and is crucial in the rounding out of a scene, and in the developing of character in a play. It is the through line of thought which holds a character together in his relations with the other characters.

14   The verb is 'what'. The super-objective is 'why'. You should find that the combination automatically releases a 'how' without you needing other props. It is the basis of improvisation. But now complicate matters.

15   Use gibberish to do any of the improvisation games you have already tried. This should release you from verbal concerns.

16   Use one single sound and vary it, using any of the games.

17   Mime the entire scene without the use of sound.

18   Without acting out the scene, sit still and recite what you would be doing if you were on stage. 'Now I come in through the door and pick up the telegram from the table. I sit down to read it. I let it drop from my fingers.... The audience should still ask and answer the usual questions at the end.

19   By this time you should have a 'what', 'why' and 'who' in all your scenes: verb, super-objective and character.

20   Improvise a scene which shows where you are, without using objects.

SANS SOUCI THEATRE,
Leicester Place, Leicester Square.

FOR THE BENEFIT OF

Mrs. SELBY.

On WEDNESDAY, APRIL 16th, 1834,

The Performances will commence with the Comedy of

Charles the Second

King Charles the Second, Mr. WILLING,   Rochester, Mr. MOGG,
Edward, (a Page) Miss JAMES, - - - - - Captain Copp, Mr. T. F. MATTHEWS.
Lady Clara, Miss MASON,   Mary Copp, Miss NETTLE.

"THE LITTLE DRUMMER!" (in Character) by Miss WALLER WYBROW.
A PAS SEUL, by Miss JAMES.
A COMIC SONG, by Mr. T. F. MATTHEWS.

After which, a Mono-Dramatic Entertainment, written expressly for Mrs. SELBY, consisting of Facts and Scraps, Illustrations of Character, &c. interspersed with Songs, entitled

THALIA'S SKETCH BOOK.

The Manageress, an eccentric lady .... Mrs. SELBY.
Mrs. Tantivy, a neck-or-nothing lady. .... Mrs. SELBY.
Mrs. Mayoress, a fat lady, ... Mrs. SELBY.
Lady Darville, an old lady, ... Mrs. SELBY.
Miss Simper, a Stage-struck lady, ... Mrs. SELBY.

The whole Performed and Represented by Mrs. SELBY.

INTRODUCTION:

Apology for being Singular—First appearance on any Stage—Dressing in Character—Stage Fright—Foundling of the Forest—Managerial Advice—Trip to Southend.

ILLUSTRATION I.---THE MANAGERESS, AN ECCENTRIC LADY.

Penny Pies---Beer and Candles---The only Juliet on the Stage---"Double, Double, toil and trouble."---Lady Macbeth and Hecate---Mrs. Jor...---Emily Worthington---Stephen Harrowby---Mrs. Siddons---How Plays are acted at Covent Garden.

Song.—THE SHORT COMPANY.

Benefit Making---The Lady's Bespeak---The Art of Pleasing---Lady Patronesses---Promotion---Kitchen and Parlour.

ILLUSTRATION II.---Mrs. MAYORESS, A FAT LADY.

The Genteel Thing---How to keep up the Spirits---Advice to Clowns---Favorite Ballads---How a Play ought to conclude---Fire, Water, Ghost, &c.

ILLUSTRATION III.---Mrs. TANTIVY, A NECK-OR-NOTHING LADY.

The Subscription Pack---Whipping-in---Tom Smith---Eccentricity of Character---New Songs---Music and Taste.

Song.—WHEN STARS ARE SHINING BRIGHT LOVE.

Appeal to the Feelings---Mind your Eye---Female Fugilists---How to avoid Scolding.

ILLUSTRATION IV.---LADY DARVILLE, AN OLD LADY.

Memory---George the Third---Costume in the time of Garrick---Youth and Age---The Diamond Necklace---Old Gentlemen---Pea Green Hat and Feathers---Plymouth---North Corner---Embarkation of Troops for Navarino---Leave-Taking---The Soldier Parting from his Wife.

Song.—I'LL THINK OF THEE.

Essay on the Passions—Passion for Acting.

ILLUSTRATION V.---Miss SIMPER, A STAGE-STRUCK YOUNG LADY.

Fluent Delivery—Romeo and Juliet---Utility of Action and Attitude---Requisites for Genteel Comedy---How to Sing with Taste and Expression.

Song.—THE SWEET SMILE.

Comfort in Misfortune---Affecting Story of the Savoyard and his Monkey---Wanderings to the Country---First Appearance in London.

CONCLUDING ADDRESS.

Song.—"Bound 'Prentice to a Coasting Ship," followed by A HORNPIPE,
By Mr. W. WILKINS.

"OYSTERS, SIR," by Miss WALLER WYBROW.

"THE SWISS TOY GIRL," by Mrs. SELBY.

A CALEDONIAN PAS DE DEUX, by Miss NETTLE and Miss C. NETTLE.

The whole to conclude with a laughable Farce, entitled

A DAY IN PARIS

In which Mrs. SELBY will appear in Five Characters.

Charles Wyrdham, (an Englishman, amusing himself in Paris) Mr. WILLING,
Sam, (his Servant) Mr. T. F. MATTHEWS,   Waiter at Meurice's Hotel, Mr. BROWN.
Emily Grenville, (betrothed to Wyndham) .... Mrs. SELBY!
Madame Janette, St. George, Victor, Napoleon de la Barbe. (a French Artiste) .... Mrs. SELBY!!
La Fleur, (a Tiger) .... Mrs. SELBY!!!
Miss Susannah Sophia Sophonisba Snowdrop, (a young Lady, fond of sentiment & waltzing) Mrs. SELBY!!!!
Captain Giriouette, (a young Officer, an admirer of the beauties of Paris) .... Mrs. SELBY!!!!!
Jane, (Servant to Miss Grenville) Miss GREEN.

Boxes 3s.	Pit 1s. 6d.	Gallery 1s.
Half-Price, 1s. 6d,	Half-Price, 1s.	Half-Price, 6d.

Doors open at half-past Six, and the Performance to commence at Seven precisely.
Tickets to be had at the Theatre; and of Mr. GIBSON, Pastry Cook, No. 1, Leicester Square.

C. G. Fairbrother, Printer, Exeter Court, Strand.

21 Make a random collection of objects, anything that is around or in anyone's pockets. Someone should pick three objects from the collection, at random, and give them to the two people who are to make a scene. The scene must utilize the objects in an organic sense. That is, you cannot come on and say, 'I think I'll open the tea-caddy,' just like that. But you can invent a scene where the tea caddy and an umbrella and a rubber duck all play a vital part. Difficult? Yes, of course. This exercise is intended to develop very quick thinking. It can be as surrealistic as is necessary.

22 Improvise a scene. Just before you go on stage, having made your usual preparations, someone else must take each of you aside and tell you, out of the hearing of the other, 'Behave as if Fred were Marilyn Monroe' (or whoever), and 'Behave as if Jane were Harold Wilson'. The scene must go on as prepared, but with the 'as ifs' played out in it. Jane and Fred do not know each other's 'as if', and will have to cope with very puzzling behaviour. You will need great concentration on what, why and who (your own character) for the scene to be able to continue.

23   Improvise a scene as usual. This time, someone should be sent to join you at any stage in the action. You must continue your scene and cope with the newcomer at once.

24   With two groups at once, set up two scenes in one place, and try to pass the focus from one group to another. You might like to have a fifth person make a sound which is a cue for the change to take place. The people who are, as it were, in the spotlight, must be able to find reasons for adapting when they return into the dark, and vice versa. Do not just go dead silent and freeze. Keep the scene working, but with different methods from the usual.

25   Do a scene as usual, but you are preoccupied with something that is never stated.

26   Set up a scene for everybody. There is no preparation. The first person goes on stage, decides where he is and who he is and finds a way of calling the next person on that shows this.

Each person must call up the next, until everyone is on stage.

Continue the scene for a while, and then one by one, in the reverse order of appearance, everyone should find a reason to go, until the stage is bare.

27   Without any preparation time, pull a scene out of hats. What you do is write down places on pieces of paper, and characters, and the weather, and time, and age, anything you can think of. Put the papers in different hats, or cooking basins or something. The two people pick a piece of paper out of each hat and invent a scene utilizing all the elements.

28   Do a scene as usual, but at a sound cue from the audience, reverse characters. At the next sound cue, change the place. At the next sound cue, change the time of day. Think of any other changes that might be made.

29   Do a scene as usual, but do it with blindfolds on.

30   As a final scene, have everybody involved in one scene, and make it last as long as possible. Stretch your imaginations to keep it alive when it flags. See how long you can go on.

If you wish to continue with this sort of game, I recommend Viola Spolin's book, listed in the booklist, but with the reservation that I do not agree with the idea of side-cueing.

50

7485 B   "FALSE GODS."   ROTARY PHOTO. E.C
MR. HENRY AINLEY   MISS EVELYN D'ALROY
AS "SATNI"   AS 'YAOUMA"

PROJECTS

Do two projects

For all these projects, you must include an assessment of how your work could operate in society and some brief theoretical analysis — in the form of notes unless you particularly want to write an essay — on what you consider the functions of theatre in general, or the particular form of theatre you find most interesting, to be.

Improvisation project

Combine the improvisational work you found most interesting and create a short play (improvised) based on this work. Describe it and include in that description how you felt the improvisational techniques have worked in the creation — if you found some things particularly easy or difficult — what you feel needs some other kind of work — technical or intellectual — and finally consider where you might go from the play you created. Would you, for example, continue it to create a larger play? If so, what form do you think that play would take? Would you make a written script, and polish what you did? Can you see other areas where improvisation might be useful, outside of theatre? How would you use it?

Write a play for theatre

Write a short play. Or, if you wish, sketch out the skeleton of a long play, and write just a scene or two from it. Remember that you have a certain amount of background material, possibly the family history material and dialogue projects in Unit 6 The Great Divide, or the gesture or role-dominated speech pattern projects from Unit 9 Verballistics. In fact, much of the background work to creative writing in Unit 9 could be of use here.

If you are interested in this project, but cannot get started, there are some things that could help. Most drama is based on the idea of conflict, and you could use conflict as a starting point. If you tried the improvisational projects, you will have experienced the power of conflict to help create living relationships between characters in even the briefest of scenes. Your play will need some sort of spine, and you might find this in historical conflicts, or in some incident in your own life which you would like to dramatize. Most playwrights start from one of these points. You could start from two characters in whom you are interested. Another way to overcome that apparently unresolvable decision on subject matter would be to use a novel or poem or painting: choose a passage that interests you in another medium and translate it into theatrical terms. Add to it as you do this. If you choose this approach, your work should be accompanied by a note saying what the original medium for the idea was, and why you chose that particular piece.

In fact, any work of this sort should be accompanied by materials or notes which help to explain the process you underwent in constructing it. This in turn will help you to assess whether you feel you have succeeded in doing what you wanted, or not. Mention anything about scenery, or type of theatre to be played in, that you feel will add to understanding of the piece. I do not expect you to write Shavian prefaces, but try to find a style of writing that suits your play.

Write a radio play

Many of the suggestions for writing a play for theatre may help you with this play, but remember that you will have to concentrate on voices and sounds and music. It is difficult to write plays without having some sort of picture in the mind's eye: this is useful at all times, but do not let it mislead you into thinking that more can be grasped by a *listening* audience than is, in fact, the case. Tape record your play, and send in the tape, as well as the script, for assessment. You may have to play all the characters yourself, or you might find people to perform for you. You will probably have to create your own noises off: be inventive with sounds — a stabbing recently done for a World Service performance only sounded right when a knife was plunged into a cabbage — and do not be afraid to use music for atmosphere.

If, for some reason, you cannot tape the play, or it simply does not sound *anything* like your imagined version, then annotate your script to indicate how sounds other than voices speaking lines would operate.

Write a television play

Your writing work here will have to expand to include: the angles from which you want major parts of the action to be seen; flashbacks; changing colour tones; anything that excites you about television drama. Do not forget to include your reasons and self-assessment.

Invent a happening

Think up a happening, and work out exactly what it would involve in order to achieve a desired result. For instance, you may need extra people, planted in the environment you have chosen, to precipitate some events. They may need to make some preparations, bring certain materials with them, do particular things with their materials. Say certain things at certain times. If you can do so, perform your happening. Whether or not you do actually perform it, write a review of the real or imagined event, saying what you would have liked to have happened as a result of it, and what actually happened.

Create a piece of street theatre

You will use some of the same processes as for a happening, but it is possible you will need a more definite theme for your work.

Choose the theme, the method of presentation, the time and place, the numbers of people involved, materials necessary, preparation to gather the audience, ...

If you can perform your street play, do so.

Once again, whether a performance results or not, write a review of the event, as you would for the happening. Your reasons for choosing the particular form of the event in both cases is very important. It will clarify much of the style and action, as you work them out.

Score a theatre event

Choose a play, a classic, a new play, one you have just written, or an event you are preparing. Bear in mind work that you have done on Unit 10 Interactive Art and Play and Unit 11 Electronic Sound and make use of ideas on music and sound as part of the environment, and the possible uses of play as an activity within the performance. Your score should include notes and/or sketches of the relations between the use of space, sound, light, people, audience and actor responses — anything you wish. Include your reasons for scoring this particular theatre event in this way.

Design a play

Choose a play. Design settings, costumes, props, masks, anything necessary for it. You can paint, draw, make ground-plans, build set models out of balsa wood or cardboard, and take photographs of them, experiment with lighting the model, include pieces of materials you think suitable for costumes or sets. If the play you have chosen is well-known — *Hamlet*, for example — all we need is the name. But if you have chosen a play less engraved on the minds of people, or one you have written, a brief description of the play is essential. Your work should also be accompanied by your reasons for designing the play as you have done, and an idea of how the designs will be used by the performers. Try to find a *dramatic* means of presenting your work.

Design a theatre of the present

You may choose your brief: design either a theatre, or a theatre complex involving other activities, or an adaptation of an existing building which you would like to see used as a theatre. You may not wish to use buildings at all; your theatre can take any form. *You do not have to be an architect* — just work out what the space is to be used for, by how many people at once, how many different activities might be going on at once, what sort of given conditions you have to contend with, whether your theatre needs machinery or not — consider how flexible you would like it to be — and make *sketches* of the theatre that is the outcome of answering such questions. I do not expect detailed plans complete with exact heights of flying space above stages or numbers of cubicles in lavatories.

I am looking for an *idea* of a theatre, a feeling of what it would look like, what it would feel like to be in it. Suggest the ways your theatre might be used. Give your reasons for your designs.

Design a theatre of the future

Follow the same procedures as for the theatre of the present, but think hard about what theatre might be doing in the future (near future? distant future? on Mars in the year 3076??) and what you would like it to be doing then.

Dance project

The dance project is contained in the broadcast notes to the television programme 'Anyone Can Dance'. This project has equal status with projects in the unit itself. If you wish to have your dance work assessed, use the same procedure as for the improvisation project, combining the work you found most interesting, and describing/explaining it, noting your ideas for possible dance performance or choreography, and assessing the experience of the work, and of your ideas for where it will lead.

INFORMATION AND BOOKS

Books

Antonin Artaud (1964) *The Theatre and its Double*, trans. Victor Corti (1970), Calder & Boyars.

Julian Beck (1972) *The Life of the Theatre*, City Lights Books.

Walter Benjamin (1966) *Understanding Brecht*, trans. Anna Bostock (1973), New Left Books.

Eric Bentley (1964) *The Life of the Drama*, Methuen.

Eric Bentley (1968) *The Theory of the Modern Stage*, Penguin.

Edward Braun (1969) *Meyerhold on Theatre*, trans. Edward Braun, Methuen.

Bertolt Brecht (1963) *The Messingkauf Dialogues*, trans. John Willett (1965), Methuen.

Peter Brook (1968) *The Empty Space*, MacGibbon & Kee.

Elizabeth Burns (1972) *Theatricality*, Longman.

Elizabeth and Tom Burns (1973) *Sociology of Literature and Drama*, Penguin.

Barrett H. Clark (1918) *European Theories of the Drama*, Crown Publishers (1965).

Robert W. Corrigan (1956) *Theatre in the Twentieth Century*, Grove Press.

Edward Gordon Craig (1911) *On the Art of the Theatre*, Mercury Books (1962).

Culture and Agitation: Theatre Documents (1972) (pamphlet), Action Books.

Serge Eisenstein (1943) *The Film Sense*, trans. Jay Leyda (1968), Faber.

Martin Esslin (1961) *Brief Chronicles*, Temple Smith (1970).

Weedon Grossmith (1913) *From Studio to Stage*, Bodley Head.

Jerzy Grotowski (1968) *Towards a Poor Theatre*, trans. Eugenio Barba, Odin Teatrets Foriag.

René Hainaux (ed.) (1972) *Stage Design throughout the world*, trans. Editions Meddens, Brussels (1973), Harrap.

Ronald Hayman (1973) *The Set-up*, Eyre Methuen.

Adrian Henri (1974) *Environments and Happenings*, Thames & Hudson.

Albert Hunt (1976) *Hopes for Great Happenings: Alternatives in Education and Theatre*, Eyre Methuen.

Eugene Ionesco (1962) *Notes and Counter Notes*, trans. Donald Watson (1964), Calder.

Stephen Joseph (1967) *Theatre in the Round*, Barrie & Rockliff.

Henry Lesnick (1973) *Guerilla Street Theatre*, Bard Books/Avon.

Charles Marowitz and Simon Trussler (1967) *Theatre at Work*, Methuen

Brander Matthews (1957) *Papers on Playmaking*, Hill & Wang.

Brander Matthews (1958) *Papers on Acting*, Hill & Wang.

Allardyce Nicholl (1925) *British Drama*, Harrap (1962).

Allardyce Nicoll (1927) *The Development of the Theatre*, Harrap (1966).

Joseph Papp (1969) *William Shakespeare's 'Naked' HAMLET*, Macmillan.

'Politics and performance' *The Drama Review* (1969), vol. 13, no. 4 (T44), TDR New York University.

Elmer Rice (1959) *The Living Theatre*, Heinemann.

James Roose-Evans (1970) *Experimental Theatre*, Discus Books/Avon.

Sybil Rosenfeld (1973) *A Short History of Scene Design in Great Britain*, Blackwell.

Richard Schechner (1969) *Public Domain*, Discus Books/Avon.

Lee Simonson (1932) *The Stage is Set*, Theatre Arts Books (1963).

Richard Slade (1964) *Masks and How to Make Them*, Faber.

Marc Slonim (1961) *Russian Theatre*, Methuen.

Richard Southern (1962) *The Seven Ages of the Theatre*, Faber.

Viola Spolin (1963) *Improvisation for the Theater*, Northwestern University Press.

Evert Sprinchorn (1965) *IBSEN. Letters and Speeches*, MacGibbon & Kee.

Constantin Stanislavski (1963) *Creating a Role*, trans. Elizabeth Reynolds Hapgood (1963), Bles.

Constantin Stanislavski (1963) *An Actor Prepares*, trans. Elizabeth Reynolds Hapgood (1963), Bles.

Arthur Symons (1909) *Plays, Acting and Music*, Constable.

John Willett (1959) *The Theatre of Bertolt Brecht*, Methuen.

John Willett (1964) *Brecht on Theatre*, Methuen.

Raymond Williams (1966) *Modern Tragedy*, Chatto & Windus.

Magazines

TDR — The Drama Review — is a particularly good American magazine. It is available in some bookshops, but would probably have to be ordered.

Theatre Quarterly is also important: it is available in bookshops, or contact them at TQ Publications Ltd, 44 Earlham Street, London WC2.

Information on community groups

If you would like to know what groups are working in your area, the Regional Arts Associations and the Arts Council itself keep up-to-date lists of the groups that receive subsidy of any kind. Your local council may also be able to help with this sort of inquiry.

ILLUSTRATIONS

Outside covers: 'Nobody loves a fairy when she's forty' (Gatehouse Gaieties old time music hall, 1975). Title page, page 6 & 25: **Endgame** (Samuel Beckett, Young Vic, designer Anushia Nieradzik). Page 7 and 40: Fitzrovia street festival. Page 8 and 9: **A Streetcar Named Desire** (Tennessee Williams, Glasgow Citizens' Theatre, 1970, designer Philip Prowse). Page 10, 11, 14 and top of 18: Cartoon Archetypical Slogan Theatre, 1965–1976. Page 12 and 13: **The Fire Raisers** (rehearsals, 1976, Gatehouse) Page 44, top right: The Maid in **The Fire Raisers**, with severed head and mirror. Page 50: Scenes from **The Fire Raisers** (performance). Page 15: Interpreting the news. Page 16: **The White Devil** (John Webster, Glasgow Citizens' Theatre, 1971, designer Philip Prowse). Page 18 (lower left): David Garrick as Macbeth, 1776 illustration. Page 19: Sarah Bernhardt as Hamlet, 1899. Page 20, 38 middle left, 49 and 56: **The Homecoming** (Harold Pinter, Gatehouse 1969, in the round). Page 21: **The Royal Hunt of the Sun** (Peter Schaffer, Greek style amphitheatre at Minack Open Air Theatre, Cornwall. Gatehouse production 1975). Page 22: New Games. Page 23: Making up. Page 26: Football crowd. Page 28, 29, 32, 52, 53, 54 and 55: Degree ceremony. Page 31: The new National Theatre. Page 33: Old people asleep. Page 34: Eton wall game, 1910. Page 35: New Games. Page 36: The Assassination of President Kennedy, the real thing (on tv) and the re-enactment by TRUTH Co & Ant Farm 1976. Page 38 (top): At a gambling club; (middle right): **Each in his own way** (Pirandello, Edinburgh 1968. Two young men made up as two very old men); (centre of 38 and 39): 'To cheer him up and help him on his way', Gatehouse Gaieties, 1975. Page 39 (top): rehearsal of **Woyzeck** (Buchner, BBC 1976); (bottom): rehearsals of **The Grand Inquisitor** (from Dostoevsky's **The Brothers Karamazov**, BBC 1976). Page 41: **Six Characters in Search of an Author** (Pirandello, Manchester 1963). Page 42 and 43: **Mother Courage and her children** (Bertolt Brecht, Berliner Ensemble production). Page 44 (top left), page 46 (bottom), inside back cover: Gatehouse Gaieties 1975, 'I may be poor but I'm honest', 'Sing sweet bird' (cod opera), and 'if I were not upon the stage, something else I'd like to be'. Page 44 and 45: Topping out ceremony. Page 45 (top): People in a pub. Page 46 (top): improvising a dance to a computer. Page 47: Sans Souci playbill, 1834; note Mrs Selby played almost all the parts. Page 48 (top): **The Chairs** (Ionesco, Middle East 1966). The other characters are created from thin air, as the chairs are brought on, (bottom): Dockers fighting for work. Page 51: **False Gods** (c.1910). Page 52 (centre): The Swan Theatre. Johann de Witt's drawing. Page 53 (centre): Interior of the Venice Theatre, a classical auditorium for the audience to watch each other. Page 58: Ancient Greek masks.

ACKNOWLEDGEMENTS FOR ILLUSTRATIONS

'Nobody loves a fairy when she's forty' and **Royal Hunt of the Sun**—Rita Triesman. Fitzrovia street festival—Angela Chadfield. National Theatre—Denys Lasdun & Partners. Eton Wall Game—The Mansell Collection. Bernhardt as Hamlet—Royal Shakespeare Theatre. Garrick as Macbeth—Victoria and Albert Museum. Football crowd—Popperfoto. Human reactions (page 37, centre picture)—Dr Hans Hass. **Mother Courage**—(page 42, left) Hainer Hall; (page 42, right) Vera Tenschert; (page 43) Percy Paukschta. People in a pub—Chris Schwartz. Swan Theatre—Victoria and Albert Museum. Venice Theatre—The Mansell Collection. Ancient Greek Masks—The Mansell Collection. Dockers fighting—Radio Times Hulton Picture Library. Interpreting the news/Glasgow Citizens' Theatre—John Barr. San Souci playbill, **The Fire Raisers**, **The Homecoming**, **The Chairs**, **Six Characters in Search of an Author**, **False Gods**, and other Gatehouse Gaieties—Susan Triesman.

THE ART AND ENVIRONMENT COURSE TEAM

Simon Nicholson (*Chairperson*)
Christopher Cornford
Christopher Crickmay
Barry Cunliffe
Katherine Dunn
Kristina Hooper
Richard Orton
David Stea
Susan Triesman
Janet Woollacott

John Barr (*Course Assistant*)
Phillipe Duchastel (*IET*)
Pam Higgins (*Designer*)
Caryl Hunter-Brown (*Liaison Librarian*)
Don Hurtley (*Staff Tutor*)
John Kenward (*Assistant Staff Tutor*)
Maureen MacKenzie (*Secretary*)

BBC

Richard Callanan
Andrew Crilly (*Co-ordinating Producer*)
John Selwyn Gilbert
Donald Holms
Noella Smith
Nat Taylor
Nancy Thomas

Programme Consultants

Hugh Davies
Mark Francis
Edward Goldsmith
Roger Hart
Bernard Leach
Ray Lorenzo
Chrissy Maher
Marion Milner
Eric Mottram
Stephanie Roberts
Colin Ward
Ken Worpole

'The Great Divide' Collective

Kathy Henderson
Maureen McCue
Michelene Wandor

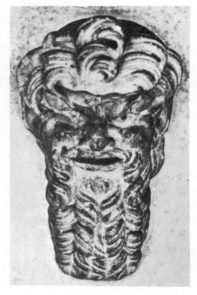

ART AND ENVIRONMENT

Unit 1   The empty box
Unit 2   Our conversation with things and places
Unit 3   Natural sound
Unit 4   Art and everyday life
Unit 5   Imaging and visual thinking
Unit 6   The great divide: The sexual division of labour, or 'Is it art?'
Unit 7   Social relationships in art
Unit 8   The moving image
Unit 9   Verballistics
Unit 10 Interactive art and play
Unit 11 Electronic sound
Unit 12 Body, mind, stage and street
Unit 13 Boundary shifting
Unit 14 Environmental mapping
Unit 15 Design with nature?
Unit 16 Art and political action

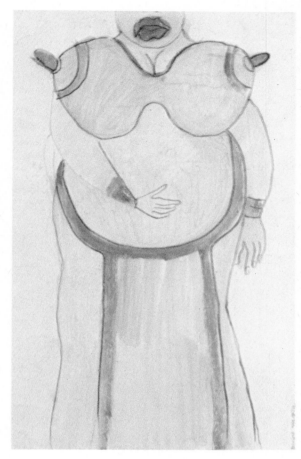

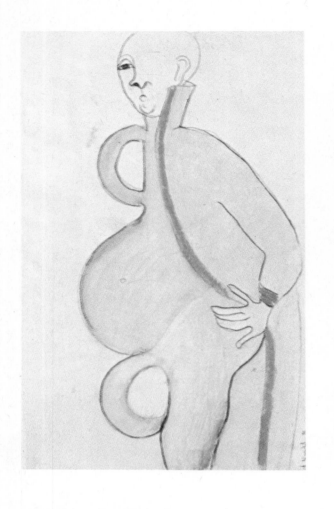 

 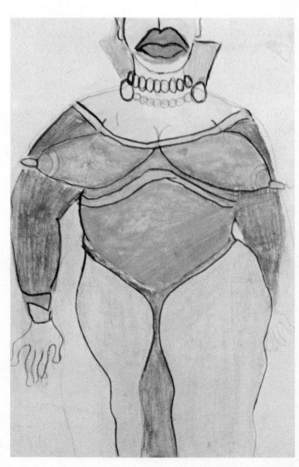